SPALDING.

Youth league BASEBALL

Coaching and Playing

SKIP BERTMAN

MASTERS PRESS

A Division of Howard W. Sams & Co.

Published by Masters Press
(A Division of Howard W. Sams & Co.)
2647 Waterfront Parkway E. Dr.
Suite 300
Indianapolis, IN 46214

10 9 8 7 6

Printed in the United States of America

Library of Congress Cataloging-in-Publication Data

Bertman, Skip.
  Youth league baseball: coaching and playing /Skip Bertman.
        p.   cm. -- (Spalding sports library)
        Reprint. Previously published: North Palm Beach, FL:
        Athletic Institute; [St. Louis, MO]: Distributed by the Sporting
        News, © 1989.
        Includes index.
        ISBN: 0-940279-68-1
        1. Baseball for children -- Coaching. 2. Baseball -- Coaching
        I. Title. II. Series.
[GV88.4.B486 1989]   93-1797
796-357'07'7 --dc 20   CIP

CREDITS:
Front cover photo of Andrew Montieth by Stephen Baker
Background photo provided by the Indianapolis Indians
Cover design by Michele Holden

The Better Sports for Kids Program

The Better Sports for Kids program is the proud mission of the National Youth Sports Coaches Association (NYSCA) which was created in 1981 to help improve out-of-school sports for over 20 million youth under the age of 16.

The non-profit association's staff of professionals work to implement a variety of programs, all in cooperation with national, state, and local associations.

The Better Sports for Kids program and its wide range of services help parents and kids get the most out of their participation in youth sports through programs such as the National Youth Sports Coaches Association national certification program for coaches, the National Association of Youth Leagues which helps leagues with all their needs in running a youth league organization, the All-American Drug-Free Team program which joins coaches and players in a drug education and prevention program, and the early introduction to lifetime sports through programs such as Hook a Kid on Golf.

The NYSCA is pleased to endorse the Spalding Youth League Series as an informative selection of coaching materials for youth coaches who wish to provide quality instruction and promote self esteem on and off the playing field.

NYSCA
National Youth Sports
Coaches Association

About the Author

Louisiana State head baseball coach Skip Bertman's association with baseball programs at all levels has spanned over 30 years. Since becoming the coach of the Tigers in 1983, Bertman's on-the-field progress has been exceptional, with LSU posting a 72.6 winning percentage, the highest in school history. In only 10 years, Bertman, the all-time winningest coach in the 100-year history of LSU baseball with a 483-182-1 record, has directed the Tigers to two NCAA championships and five Southeastern Conference titles.

With a combination of winning baseball and successful promotions, in addition to a strong commitment from the University, Bertman and LSU have enjoyed incredible success, rising from a fifth-place SEC finish in his first season in 1984 to an SEC title and the school's first-ever College World Series appearance in 1986. Bertman has guided LSU to the College World Series in six of the last eight seasons, and the Tigers claimed the national champion- ship in 1991 and 1993. In addition, nearly 100 percent of the athletes who played four years at LSU have gone on to attain their degrees, and coach Bertman has had over 200 of his players advance into the professional ranks.

Table of Contents

Foreword 1

I.   **Start Them When They're Young** 5

II. **The Catcher** 11

    Equipment 11
    Positioning and Giving Signs 13
    Stance, Target and Receiving the Ball 15
    Handling the Low Pitch 20
    Throwing 22
    Protecting Home Plate 28
    Catching the Pop Fly 30
    General Information 31

III. **The Pitcher** 35

    Stance and Delivery 36
    The Set or Stretch Position 42
    The Pitcher as a Fielder 45
    Control and the Various Pitches 46
    General Information 52

IV. **The First Baseman** 57

    Getting to the Bag 57
    Fielding Ground Balls 61
    Handling Bunts 63
    Holding the Runner On 64
    Catching Pop Flies 65
    Cutoff and Relay Position 65
    General Information 67

V. **The Third Baseman** 71

    The Glove 72
    Positioning and Fielding Ground Balls 72

Bunt Situations 76
Tags and Cutoffs 77
General Information 78

VI. **The Second Baseman** 83

Catching the Ball 83
Stance and Basic Fielding Position 84
Fielding Ground Balls 85
Making the Double Play 86
The Double Cutoff 89
Rundowns 90
General Information 91

VII. **The Shortstop** 95

Stance and Basic Fielding Position 95
Fielding Ground Balls 97
Making the Double Play 100
Communication 100
The Appeal Play 102
General Information 103

VIII. **The Outfielder** 107

Stance and Basic Positioning 108
Catching the Ball 109
Communication 112
Fielding Ground Balls and Throwing 113
General Information 115

IX. **Hitting and Bunting** 119

Bat, Grip and Stance 120
Stride and Swing 124
Use of the Batting Tee 133
General Information 134
Bunting 137

X. **Baserunning and Base Coaching** 145

Qualifications of a Good Base Runner 145
Running from Home Plate 146
Leading Off the Various Bases 147

Stealing the Various Bases 152
Sliding 154
Baserunning Plays 158
Coaching the Bases 160
Signals 162
General Information 164

XI. **Practice Organization and Drills** 167

Batting Practice 169
Play Situations 171
Other Drills and Suggestions 172
Drills, Drills, Drills! 176

Fault Correction Index 179

Foreword

No man ever stands so tall as when he stoops to help a boy. Coaching is a privilege; we owe the youngsters our best effort. I feel privileged indeed to have been able to teach and coach so many fine young people. Being close to baseball and youngsters has brought many heartwarming and satisfying experiences. I am sure the same will follow for you.

Each chapter of the book is devoted to a specific phase of the game. All the positions are covered, one at a time. The chapters concerning the specific positions cover basic skills such as throwing and catching as well as more complex matters such as position fundamentals. These chapters also deal with related points ranging from proper footwear to rundown execution. Other skills, such as hitting and bunting, baserunning and base coaching, and drills and practice organization, are covered in separate chapters.

Throughout the book references will be made to "upper" and "lower" divisions. The lower division includes youngsters seven to ten years of age. The upper division includes youngsters aged eleven to fourteen. For the most part the information may be used for youngsters seven through fourteen. However, some drills emphasize skills that the younger players are not ready to master. Of course each youngster is different; some variations of the drills might be necessary for coaches and certain players to reach desired results.

The book also has a unique feature called a "fault-correction" index. I have tried to point out the most common faults of youth-leaguers in all areas of the game. The index lists these faults alphabetically and cites the pages that include the procedures to correct them. For example, if you have a boy who steps in the bucket when he bats, you can look under "steps in the bucket" to locate the corrective measures.

All the boys in the photographs are members of the Millerville Phillies and have either attended my baseball camp or played in a league where I have given several clinics about the game of baseball. Most of them have been to my camp several times. They are not superstars. Most are just average ball players like the majority of your team. I believe that all these boys and others were helped by the techniques and information in this book. I'm sure your players can benefit as well. Through you, they can gain the instruction and confidence necessary to have a wonderful youth-league baseball experience.

Dedicated to:

All youth league coaches and their families, but especially mine : my wife, Sandy, and my four daughters, Jan, Jodi, Lisa, and Lori.

Special thanks to:

The many individuals who helped make this book possible. All the coaches and players who have helped me learn about the game and the boys who gave hours of their time posing for photographs. Thanks also goes to Jim Wells and Randy Davis, two of my assistant coaches, who helped me write this book.

league Youth BASEBALL

I. Start Them When They're Young

Babe Ruth once said, "Start them when they're young. Teach them to play when they're four years old." Youngsters learn something about baseball even before the youth-league coach starts his first practice session. They throw with their fathers, attempt to hit the ball, run around imaginary bases and enjoy every second of it.

In just a few short years these youngsters will be on youth-league baseball teams that will be a community effort, teaching moral and spiritual values, molding character, and improving physical fitness through wholesome recreation.

No one knows exactly how many youngsters play baseball each year. Little League Inc. alone has over 2.5 million participants aged nine to eighteen in twenty-eight countries. Many other leagues have charters and belong to programs with national offices, like Khoury League, Babe Ruth, Boys Baseball and Dixie Youth-League, to name a few. Many other youngsters play in leagues that have rules similar to those of the national organizations but do not actually have charters. As new leagues develop, fewer and fewer youngsters are playing pickup games in sandlots without adult supervision.

Regardless of their ages and where they play, all youngsters want to improve their playing ability and find success. Most leagues provide for a coach and/or manager for each team to help every youngster attain these goals. It is for these coaches and managers, as well as for all youth-league participants, that this book is written.

I once heard a local radio editorial degrading the area youth-league programs by sarcastically asking, "How many ex-major leaguers are coaching these kids?" Make no mistake about it—professional baseball experience is not necessary to be a successful youth-league coach. In fact, it might even be harmful. A youth-league baseball game is not a miniature version of the Chicago Cubs vs. the St. Louis Cardinals. Coaches with professional baseball backgrounds tend to teach major-league baseball rather than youth-league baseball. But, in addition to the obvious physical differences between the participants, of professional baseball and youth-league baseball, the games are different in themselves.

A regulation diamond has the bases set ninety feet apart. It has been like this since 1845, when Alexander Cartwright laid out the first diamond. Changing the distance between the bases changes the delicate balance and subtleties of the game. A steal of any base is usually a very close play. An infield double play usually just gets the runner at first base. The runner trying to score from second base on a single to the outfield normally has just enough time to make it to home plate. On a smaller youth-league field the symmetry is not the same. Fast runners steal with relative ease. Double plays are rare, and because the outfielders play shallow, a runner can have trouble scoring from second on a base hit.

The strategy of the youth-league game differs in many instances from that of professional baseball. For example, a major-league runner is more likely to be sacrificed to second, whereas in youth-league baseball he's more apt to steal. A major-league runner would rarely steal third base with two outs, figuring that he is already in scoring position at second and a hit will score him anyway. But in a youth-league game an exceptionally weak hitter might be up and a hit very unlikely. Certainly a youth-league runner would rather be at third base because of the ever-present possibility of the passed ball or wild pitch.

Another example of the difference in strategy is the choice of the cutoff man on throws to home plate from the outfield. While the first baseman is used on most regulation fields, the pitcher is probably better suited for this on a youth-league field. On a regulation field the pitcher has the responsibility of backing up a throw to home plate. Youth-league diamonds usually have the backstops so close to home plate that backing up the throw is unnecessary. In addition, the pitcher is probably the best athlete on the field and should handle as many balls as possible.

Still another reason for the difference between professional and youth-league baseball strategy is that youth-league games last four to seven innings, whereas the pros play nine innings. Don't think you're hurting a boy's chances for a professional career because your methods may differ from major-league methods. Most of the players from your league will never play in high school, let alone the major leagues. There are only about six hundred major-leaguers at any time. That's far less than one-tenth of one percent of the population of our society—a very select group indeed. Certainly, serving as farm systems for higher baseball is a very minor reason for the existence of youth baseball leagues. Besides, players with unique baseball talent who have professional potential will be flexible enough to meet any coaching situation.

Naturally, some coaches will be better than others but if they are it's because they're more involved and really enjoy what they're doing and not necessarily because they outfox the other coaches. Out of the days of trial and error, success and failure, and long hours of practice and effort come the skills to play the game. For some, the skills come easily; they learn fast and almost without effort. For most, the game is tough, and skill is gained slowly and painfully. For some, unfortunately, skill never comes.

Teams from Taiwan have won most of the recent Little League World Series. Most of these teams were coached by schoolteachers, but more important, most of the players practiced every day, averaging forty swings in batting practice and forty ground balls or fly balls on defense. The Chinese coaches didn't outsmart their coaching counterparts, but they may have outworked them. While this type of practice session isn't necessary, and overworking players is obviously not right, I mention the Taiwanese teams to show that if coaches expect well-played baseball they must work at achieving it. There are no tips that will make coaching baseball at any level an easy job.

I'm not advocating overcoaching. Don't try to teach everything to every player. You don't want to sap the fun out of the game by placing too much pressure on the youngsters. But every coach wants to be able to offer his players sound fundamental baseball techniques. A coach wants to help a boy when he's not doing well by giving him proper advice that will help him find success.

Early in his career every youth-league player learns his first lesson of failure and defeat. Have each youngster hold his head high and accept defeat graciously, learning a lesson from the loss that will pave the way to victory.

More than anything else a coach needs compassion. He must continually encourage his players. If a coach takes his responsibility to the players seriously but never takes himself too seriously, he'll do fine. Feel very proud when your ambition is met by seeing your team play better each time they take the field. This, plus the fact that the youngsters enjoyed themselves, makes every coach who really cares a winner.

Every coach must promote spirit. Spirit is that quality which enables a player to play better than he is physically capable of playing. Spirit is like a disease; it's contagious. Every coach owes it to his players to keep the "disease" spreading from player to player, to the fans and to the community.

A coach and his players must have courage and self-reliance. The coach must do what he knows to be right regardless of what the fans or opponents might think. Of course you must be prepared for the fans with twenty-twenty hindsight. They always know what to do after the game has been played. Second-guessing is usually harmless and should not be taken personally. Your decisions will not always work out for the best, of course, but if they are based on what you think is best for your boys, then they are 100 percent correct. No coach or player can compromise any principles and still reach the goals of successful youth-league participation.

If you care enough to purchase a book that will help, then you're already halfway there. I, too, want to help. If any part of the book needs further explanation, or if I can be of any assistance, please call or write to me at the address listed on the copyright page.

II. The Catcher

The catcher is, more often than not, the team leader. Part quarterback, part evangelist, the holler guy, a traffic director, part psychiatrist, he is usually the most knowledgeable player on the field. Not only does he work closely with the pitcher, but he also helps everyone else, as he is the only player on the field who can see the other eight positions.

There is always a shortage of catchers at every level of baseball. Probably the main reason for the chronic scarcity is not the physical demand of the position but the common misconception that catchers come in certain shapes and sizes. Most youth-league coaches place the youngster with the most innate athletic skill on the mound or at shortstop. All too often the heavy youngster who can't run well is placed behind the plate. The really talented youngsters become infielders or pitchers, never realizing that they might have developed into excellent catchers.

Many youngsters and parents fear catching as physically dangerous. However, the catcher who knows proper fundamentals and uses proper equipment isn't any more likely to get injured than an infielder except by foul tips. Playing even a few years as a catcher can help a youngster gain baseball knowledge that he can use later at any position. An alert catcher will also pick up knowledge concerning hitting as he watches the varied styles of opposing batters.

Because so few players become catchers, coaches with catching experience are very rare. However, any willing coach can help a youngster who has the desire to play one of the toughest positions in all of sports.

Equipment

Youth-league catchers should use a mitt with a break or hinge (Fig. 2-1). It makes for easier receiving. Naturally, the mitt should be used often before the season begins so that it will not be too rigid. The only way to properly break in a glove is to use it often in practice sessions. Many youth-league catchers break the webbing of their mitts because they catch the ball there instead of in the pocket. Most sporting-goods stores can supply lace and have their personnel fix

Fig. 2-1. *Proper equipment for catchers includes all of the above.*

the webbing in a very short while. Should a catcher constantly catch the ball in the webbing, have him warm up with an old mitt that has no webbing until he gets the idea of catching the ball in the pocket. If the commissioner of your league does not object, paint the pocket of the mitt white. This not only helps the catcher think "pocket" but also provides a better target for the pitcher.

If the catcher does not catch the ball with two hands and appears to be the victim of too many passed balls, have him warm up with the newest and most rigid mitt you can find. The ball will pop out of the new mitt unless he uses two hands. When a catcher uses one of the special mitts or just warms up a pitcher, **he should be wearing his mask**. This is not only a safety measure but helps him avoid bad habits like turning his head on low balls that bounce in front of him. Remember, catchers in both the lower division (ages seven to ten) or the upper division (ages eleven to fourteen) should be catching almost every pitch with two hands.

At times, a catcher will complain that his hand hurts from catching the ball in the pocket. For a bone bruise on the catching hand, protection is available in many forms. During a ball game, the catcher can place a soft-drink cup with the bottom punched out inside the mitt in front of his hand. Commercial sponges are available in sporting-goods stores. My favorite protection pad is one that the coach makes himself with gauze pads and adhesive tape. Covering the gauze pads carefully with the tape offers protection without the resiliency of the sponge. A commercial golf glove can also be used. Many catchers will catch with the index finger outside the mitt. This not only protects against bone bruises but should give the youngster more control of his catcher's mitt as well.

The mask, of course, must be of top quality. Once again, it should be used by all catchers when warming up pitchers before games or during practice sessions. The wire mask is too heavy for lower-division catchers. It may offer better vision, but the correct fit is almost impossible for most lower-division youngsters. A bar mask made of steel or magnesium will be fine so long as the fit is proper. Replacement padding and harness straps are available for every model mask. All straps are adjustable, so the fit can be made with a bar mask on even the smallest catcher. A catcher's helmet is a **must**. If the league rule does not require helmets, you make sure your catcher wears one anyway. There are many models available, and most are adjustable. Some even attach to the mask. The helmet protects the catcher from the bat when it is unintentionally let go or when the hitter misses a high-and-inside pitch and lets go of the bat with the top hand.

The chest protector is another piece of equipment in which the fit is the most important item of all. Many youth protectors are too large and offer very little protection just below the neck. Make sure the chest protector is worn high enough and tight enough to offer total protection. A chest protector does not need an extension pad below the waist to protect the groin if the catcher wears a protective cup and proper supporter. Youth-league cups and supporters are available, although it is very difficult to get lower-division catchers to wear them. If the catcher does not use a cup, make sure he has a chest protector with an extension pad.

Shin guards are often worn on the wrong legs. The clips belong on the outside of the leg. Because they are easier to put on with the clips on the inside, most young catchers put them on that way and no one tells them differently. The clips can get caught together when worn that way, and the player may fall. Make sure the shin guard covers the instep all the way up to the knee, and on upper-division catchers, even above the knee. Straps on most shin guards are adjustable. However, if the shin guard appears to be too large, the top and middle straps can be crossed, making a tighter fit for the catcher who has a small frame.

Positioning and Giving Signs

To give signals properly (for upper-division players), or while resting between pitchers for younger ones, the catcher should squat with his feet close together (Fig. 2-2). The toes are pointed slightly inward to keep the knees from spreading too wide and allowing the first- or third-base coach to see the signals. The mitt hangs loosely over the knee. A common mistake of youth-league catchers is giving signals too low. Another is tipping off the signals by moving the elbow to give different signs.

For catchers giving signs, the simplest system is the digit method, with one finger meaning fastball, two meaning curve, and three meaning change-up. Shaking all the fingers could indicate a fourth pitch or a specific defensive play. A fist is usually the signal for a pitch-out (a fastball, usually high and outside so the batter cannot hit it and the catcher is able to throw to a base to get a runner).

Sometimes playing at night or catching a pitcher who has poor vision makes the digit system difficult. A set of signs for these conditions could be touching the mask for a fastball, the chest protector for a curve, and a shin guard for a change-up. The catcher should use fingers as a decoy so the offensive team will not pick up his other method of giving signals.

Pick-off signals are not necessary in the lower division. However, for those catchers skilled enough at the upper levels, signals with the first and third basemen are common. These signals are taking the glove off and holding it in the other hand, shouting the number of outs to the catcher, and touching various parts of the uniform and/or body. The only teaching point here is that the infielder should usually give the first signal: if he does not, he must return the catcher's signal to be certain someone will always be covering the base.

The coach must encourage the players to try new signals, letting them make up their own. Take time off from a phase of practice and

Fig. 2-2. *Good position for giving signals.*

let the players sit around and talk about signals. You'll be surprised at what they can come up with.

Be careful not to let your catcher or other players overreact in attempting to hide signals. Sometimes the catcher will give his signals too fast or hide them with his mitt, and the pitcher will be confused. Only the aforementioned precautions are necessary to prevent the opposition from seeing the catcher's signals.

Stance, Target and Receiving the Ball

After the sign has been given or if no sign is used (in most lower-division play), the receiver must immediately get into a crouching position. He should not wait for the pitcher to start winding up. This crouching position should be used whether or not there are base-runners. This allows the pitcher to use the catcher's mitt, shin guards, mask, or whole body for his target. It also puts the catcher in a better position to receive the pitch wherever it is thrown. All catchers can get into the good crouch position, which is demonstrated in Figure 2-3. Even lower-division catchers can attain this position by constant

Fig. 2-3. *The catcher is close enough when his glove is just behind the batter's back elbow.*

practice. The elbows should be outside the knees, and the feet should be slightly wider than the shoulders. The right foot should be a little further back than the left foot, and the toes of the right foot should be pointed toward the second baseman. It is important for the catcher to be comfortable. Catchers who lack confidence in their crouch positions often lose strikes by jumping up in front of the umpire and blocking his vision.

A chair may be necessary to teach young catchers the proper position (Fig. 2-4). Use the chair each day until the catcher realizes that flexibility in the thigh is the necessary ingredient of the "target" stance. Another method of starting off a young catcher is to have him take a football lineman's stance. From this position he slowly rocks back into the proper crouch.

A position that can be used with no runners on base to get the pitcher to throw the ball lower is by having the catcher kneel on his left knee and extend his right leg (e.g. Tony Pena, St. Louis Cardinals). Again, this stance should only be used with no runners on base and for the pitcher who needs a lower target.

Many youth-league catchers catch too far away from the hitter. A good catcher at any level catches as close as possible to the batter in an effort to save more strikes, to let fewer balls bounce, and to catch more foul tips. While there is not a set distance, the catcher and coach will soon learn they can move up closer to the batter as long as the catcher does not reach for the ball. The only hitter the catcher

Fig. 2-4. *The chair is a good teaching tool for the "Target Stance."*

must watch for is the youngster who swings extremely late or steps back with his rear foot before swinging. Under normal conditions the catcher should be able to get as close as shown in Figure 2-3. Remember, the catcher who works close to the hitter can catch more foul tips and have fewer balls bounce in front of him. He can also help his pitcher get more strikes called (Diagram 2-1). He is also safer physically, because he is less likely to get hit with a batted ball on his bare hand.

Much has been written about protecting the meat hand from a foul tip. Actually the only catcher who is totally protected is the one-hand catcher. While catching with one hand may be adequate in professional ball, youth-league catchers **should not** copy the professionals in this instance. Catching the ball with two hands is necessary when trying to throw out a base runner who's stealing. The best way for a young catcher to protect his bare hand is to fold it (but not make a clenched fist) with the thumb behind the fingers, which should be relaxed and pointed toward the ground (Fig. 2-5).

There are some important teaching points to help the catcher receive each pitch with a minimum chance of being hit by a foul tip. One, all pitches from about the knees up should be caught with the thumbs together (fingers pointing up); two, all low pitches should be caught with the little fingers together (fingers pointing toward the ground).

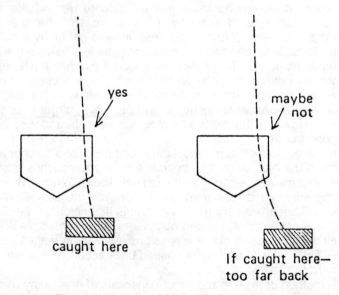

yes

caught here

maybe
not

If caught here—
too far back

Diagram 2-1. *The pitch that should be called a strike but if caught too far back tends to look more like a ball to the umpire.*

Fig. 2-5. *The bare hand is in a safe position: folded, the thumb behind the fingers, which are pointed toward the ground.*

Be careful not to catch the ball as shown in Figure 2-6, with the heels of the hands together. Here the fingers are exposed, and the foul tip will inevitably hit the bare hand. Another teaching point that every coach must emphasize is that the catcher who hustles after every ball, attempts to keep his body in front of the ball, and concentrates on every pitch is also less likely to get hit by a foul tip.

The mitt is placed directly behind home plate and held very still as the pitcher winds up. The pitcher can pick out the mitt, mask, either shin guard or either shoulder as his target. Some pitchers use the catcher as a whole for their targets. Working with his pitchers individually will enable a catcher to find out which target is best for each one. However, the catcher must remain very still and very low to be a good target.

There is no doubt that the most important thing for a catcher to do is to catch the ball. While this sounds trite, many coaches take for granted that the catcher will catch each ball thrown to him. When the opposing runner reaches third base, however, the danger of the passed ball becomes very real. The truth is that catchers are drilled far too little, while infielders and outfielders get ground balls and fly balls all the time during practice sessions. As a youth-league coach, you will find that wild pitches or passed balls occur more often than infield errors.

One method of making a catcher conscious of how many pitches he catches is to count the number of balls he catches and the number he drops. This can be done in batting practice or while

Fig. 2-6. *There's trouble here. The fingers are exposed when catching the ball with the palms of the hands together.*

warming up a pitcher. Another drill that is a must for all youth-league catchers in both the upper and lower divisions is what I've always called the "quick hands" drill. Here the coach or any player stands twenty-five to forty feet away from the catcher, who is in full gear and in front of a backstop or a fence. The distance is about half as far as the pitcher would be throwing during a ball game. The thrower throws the ball from this shorter distance almost as fast as the pitcher would throw it from the regulation distance. Don't be afraid to throw hard. However, soft rubber baseballs should be used for beginning catchers. Make the catcher attempt to catch all types of pitches. Start with pitches that might be strikes, then throw outside pitches, then inside. Make the catcher leave his feet to practice catching extremely high pitches. No low balls—that is, balls that bounce in front of the catcher—should be thrown; save those for another drill. This drill can be done before a game as well as during each practice session. The catcher should receive about twenty-five balls during each drill.

A similar drill to improve the catcher's hands is called the "rag ball" drill. This drill is set up just like the "quick hands" drill. The difference is that the catcher does not use a mitt and you throw rag balls or tennis balls. The catcher must catch the ball barehanded with his glove hand.

The ball that is low and away from his mitt hand is the toughest catch. Naturally this pitch should be thrown often in drills. A slight relaxation of the hands as the pitcher lets the ball go will prevent "tense" or "stiff" hands. Check to see that the fingers are in proper position as the pitch is received. Most youth-league catchers do not practice catching all types of pitches. Prevent many passed balls and stop most potential wild pitches by using the "quick hands" and the "rag ball" drills.

Handling the Low Pitch

One of the great joys in working with catchers is seeing them become proficient in blocking the pitch in the dirt. Every catcher who will work at this can become very good at it. In fact, the younger the catcher, the easier it is to teach him. First, make sure he is in full gear, including a cup or an extension pad on his chest protector. If the older catcher complains about the cup being uncomfortable, explain to him that he will get accustomed to it. Most good catchers won't even watch a game on television without a cup.

After the catcher is in full gear, have him go to work with the "low-ball" drill. Once again the catcher and the coach or his thrower go to work. Station yourself about thirty feet from the catcher and place him in the proper position to block the ball (Fig. 2-7). Throw balls that bounce a foot or two in front of him. Stress the importance of only blocking the ball and not catching it. Make sure his chin is placed against his chest protector to protect his neck, his bare hand is

Fig. 2-7. *Proper low ball position.*

behind his mitt, and his toes are pointing out so he won't fall forward. In starting out, do not have him drop into this position yet, just let him feel the sensation of blocking the ball and knowing that his equipment will protect him. When you are satisfied with his position for blocking the low ball, have him drop into it as you throw the ball (Fig. 2-8). The catcher must drop to **both knees** constantly, as this is the major factor in blocking balls in the dirt. As he blocks balls, remind him that if he turns his head he does not have the protection of the mask. Remind him as he falls to his knees that he should be on his insteps rather than the tops of his feet. This will prevent him from falling forward and leave him more likely to cushion the ball and keep it close to him after impact.

If your catcher hadn't thought about it before, he knows now that catching is the toughest position of them all. Low balls may bounce off the heel of his glove and hit the unprotected area of his arms, but no serious injury is likely to occur from blocking them. For a ball to the catcher's right, he drops to his right knee first, following quickly with the other knee to attain the low-ball position. However, here the catcher should have his right shoulder angled toward the pitcher. If his body is in proper position and the ball hits it, the ball most likely will stay in front of him. Runners are not likely to advance if the ball is in front of the catcher. If he is not angled correctly and the ball hits him, it will bounce toward first base (Diagram 2-2). The low ball to the catcher's left is handled the same way except that the left knee drops to the ground first. Once again stress body position and proper

Fig. 2-8. Catchers must drill "hands" and "low balls" thrown by a coach or teammate.

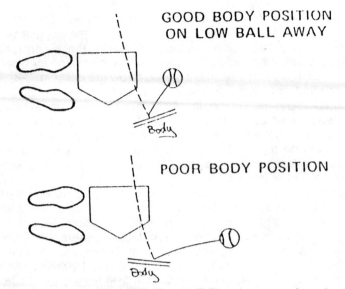

GOOD BODY POSITION
ON LOW BALL AWAY

POOR BODY POSITION

Diagram 2-2. *Stay in front of the low ball. The chest must face the pitcher.*

angle. The player or coach working the "low-ball" drill must throw all types of pitches to all locations. Make them tough to catch, just as in a game. Once again, soft rubber baseballs may be used for beginning catchers.

Remember, innate skills are not needed to block low balls. Hard work and a desire to succeed are the most important attributes for a catcher to become proficient at this crucial play.

Throwing

Gripping the ball across the seams has proven most effective for horseshoe-shaped seams. Many lower-division players must grip the ball with three fingers because their hands are too small. However, they too grip the ball across the seams whenever possible (Fig. 2-9). This gripping method applies to all players regardless of position, with the possible exception of the pitcher. The rotation of the ball when thrown will tend to keep its trajectory straight. Gripping the ball can be practiced while playing catch. The players can attempt to return the ball holding it across the seams after grabbing the ball and feeling for the seams. Lower-division players need not stress the grip. It is far more important that they concentrate on the "principle of opposition"; that is, their left foot goes forward when they throw with

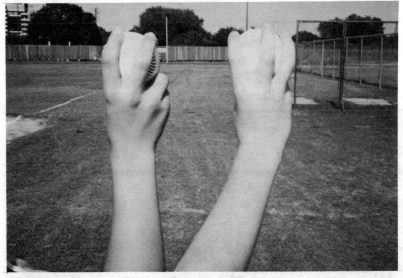

Fig. 2-9. *Proper grip for throwing the ball. Players with small hands may need three fingers.*

their right hand. They must also be told to point the toes of the front foot exactly where they want to throw the ball.

Catchers must get rid of the ball quickly. This means catching the ball with two hands. While both hands are being brought into the throwing position, the bare hand can push against the glove in order to get a good grip on the ball. The full overhand method and the more common three-quarter method shown in Figure 2-10 are the only acceptable methods of throwing for young catchers.

While strength in the throwing arm is mostly innate, throwing technique can be helped. If a player throws the ball with his elbow below his shoulder (Fig. 2-11). Chances are his throwing can be improved. One way to teach this is to have the player throw the ball while lying on his back (Fig. 2-12), the player soon realizes that the arm needs the body to help on the throw, and of course he'll have trouble throwing sidearm. For this drill the coach stands only a few feet from the player and checks throwing form as he awaits the ball. Throwing while down on one knee (Fig. 2-13) is great for warming up and also another good way to practice the throwing technique. Here the young player learns to throw by twisting his body first.

Many major-leaguers have mastered the snap throw and sidearm flip. Don't let your catcher use these throws. Even when he warms up he should be thinking about the grip and where he wants to point his toe for the return throw. A young player can injure his throwing arm by

Fig. 2-10. *Here the throwing arm is in good position.*

Fig. 2-11. *Here the throwing arm is too low.*

Fig. 2-12. *A good drill to correct "sidearm" throwing.*

Fig. 2-13. *Throwing from one knee will improve technique and strengthen the arm.*

not throwing correctly. To make the overhand throw or the more common three-quarter throw, the catcher shifts his weight to his right foot, rotates his shoulders to the right, and pushes off his right foot.

Throwing is also a matter of footwork. As all youth-league coaches learn very quickly, the steal is a very potent weapon. The sweep method is the best way for young catchers to catch and throw (Diagram 2-3). However, lower-division catchers will use another method, which I will explain later, until the sweep method can be mastered. To use the sweep method with a right-handed hitter, the catcher should take a short pivot step with his right foot on the pitch, stepping down the middle of the plate or on the outside portion of the plate. The most important thing to remember is that he does not wait until he has caught the ball to take his pivot step. Using peripheral vision, he starts movement as the pitcher releases the ball and he sees the runner leaving first to steal second base. Even if youth-league rules prohibit the runner leaving a base until the ball has passed the batter, the catcher should use this footwork. His body must be in motion at the time he catches the ball. He must attempt to stay low, move quickly, and keep good body balance. This exceptionally tough skill can only be achieved by constant practice. The coach must pitch to him so he can attempt to catch a teammate stealing in practice. Most catchers will find their own way if you let them practice enough and offer enough encouragement.

Throwing to second base is even more difficult on a very close pitch to a right-handed batter or when a left-hander is batting. Some coaches have had right-handed hitters stand up at the plate as a left-hander until the first pitch was thrown and second was stolen, and then bat right-handed. This is perfectly legal. With a left-handed

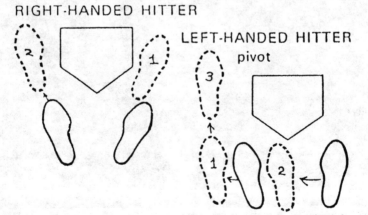

Diagram 2-3. *The sweep method of catching and throwing for left- and right-handed hitters.*

batter or a very close pitch to a right-handed hitter, the pivot is made to the left with the left foot, then the right foot is brought into position and the left foot is extended toward second base as the throw is made (see Diagram 2-3). When a lefty is batting, the catcher should follow this procedure on every pitch. With the help of the first baseman yelling "There he goes," he should be ready when the runner steals. Many times it is difficult for a catcher to see the runner break for second with a left-handed hitter standing deep in the batter's box.

In trying to stop the steal at third base, the catcher steps with his right foot toward first base. After catching the ball he shifts his weight to his right foot, extends his left foot toward third and delivers the same three-quarter or overhand throw. Once again the coach will have to set up situations in practice for the catcher to react to. Have your runners steal, have the defense react, and let the catcher make the throw.

The throw to second or third should not be placed exactly on the bag, even if the catcher could deliver the ball there. A better throw is one that is handled knee-high above the bag.

Another way to improve the catcher's throwing is to use a stopwatch. Start the watch as the ball enters the catcher's glove and stop it when it enters the second baseman's or shortstop's glove at the bag. You can get a good idea of how well the catcher can release the ball and how fast it travels. While the time on the stopwatch can only be compared to the times of the other catchers on the team and related to the specific distances you are using, the idea is to make the catcher aware of the need for getting rid of the ball quickly rather than making extremely hard throws.

Lower-division catchers usually will not be able to follow the above procedures. Actually these youngsters must catch the ball first and then "crow-hop"; that is, step with the left foot toward the base and make a hopping step with the right foot as they set to throw. This takes longer than the sweep method but is necessary to permit younger boys to reach the base without injuring their arms.

Runners on first and third base put the defense on edge, but it need not be that way. If the catcher will practice the alternatives to just holding the ball on a steal the situation can work out for the defense. The catcher takes his normal steps to throw to second, except that he must look at the runner on third before throwing the ball. If the runner at third has started home or has a large lead and is leaning toward home, the catcher will not throw to second but will adjust his feet and throw to third. The third baseman must help here; he can yell for the catcher to throw to third if he feels the runner is too far off third base.

If the runner has a short lead, or if he is going back to third and the third baseman does not yell, the throw goes through to second base. The pitcher should make believe he is going to catch the ball in order to hold the runner at third that much longer. Most youth-league catchers can throw the ball at least to a cutoff man in front of second base.

Regardless of who is at bat, the second baseman should come up about fifteen feet in front of second base. If the throw is poor, he automatically cuts it off and checks third base. If the runner holds, and the throw looks as if it will reach second base, the cutoff man allows it to go through and the shortstop catches it at the bag and tags the runner. Remember, the second baseman is only a short distance in back of the pitcher and he can return the ball home if the runner leaves from third. If the catcher elects not to throw to second because the runner at third appears to be too quick to get on the return throw from second, he may do one of the following: first, he can throw directly back to the pitcher, preferably a high throw. The pitcher catches the ball and checks the runner at third. Of course this play is more likely to work if your catcher has thrown to second base on prior similar situations. Secondly, the catcher can throw directly to third, **right now!!**, without faking or hesitating at all. Only the throw back to the pitcher needs a signal before the play; otherwise the third baseman and other infielders go to their proper places. They should always expect a throw. If the catcher wants to signal the pitcher, he should do it verbally ("take **no** chances") or use his hand, making an "**X**" on his chest protector before he signals for the pitch.

Protecting Home Plate

In tagging a runner at home plate, the catcher must remember that the runner has built up momentum. If at all possible he should avoid a collision. No catcher ever helped his team when he was home injured. Very few coaches would tell a runner to run into the catcher, but sometimes that catcher forces a showdown by not giving the runner room to slide. Giving the runner a place to slide works to the benefit of the catcher because now he'll know where the runner is going to slide. The catcher waiting to receive a throw from centerfield leaves room for the runner to slide on the third-base side (Fig. 2-14). After the runner starts his slide, the catcher holds the ball squarely in his bare hand and protects it with the glove; he kneels on his right knee and the runner slides into the tag (Fig. 2-15).

As mentioned before, the catcher should wear his mask when warming up pitchers and when taking pregame infield practice. He should wear his mask while making a play at the plate for the same reason: protection from the bad bounce. Obviously, if a catcher can

Fig. 2-14. *Leave room for the runner to slide. This is good position awaiting the throw. Catcher should keep his mask on.*

Fig. 2-15. *Good position for tag at the plate. Make sure the ball is held tightly in the bare hand and covered by the glove.*

see all the pitches with his mask on, he need not take it off for better vision on a play where the ball is thrown from the field to home plate. Catchers take their masks off for pop-ups because they are looking straight up and the bars would hinder their vision. Wearing the mask at all other times helps avoid the bad habit of turning the head on balls that bounce in the dirt, which happens often in youth-league baseball. With the mask on, the catcher will learn better fielding habits. Incidentally, for this reason the catcher should wear his gear as often as possible in practice.

Even a throw from right field or the right side of the diamond should be taken on the inside portion of home plate, leaving the runner the outside or third-base side of home plate for his slide. In no instance should the catcher straddle home plate like an infielder or run up to get the throw if it appears to be short. He must wait in this position for the ball whether it bounces or not. Catchers should be instructed to remove the bat, if possible, before the action at home plate. However, umpires should also be taught to do this, and they usually find it easier than the catcher.

If the runner misses home in an attempt to avoid the tag, don't go after him; wait for him to come back to the plate. Most umpires will call a runner out at home plate if there is contact at all. Therefore, it is not necessary to be overaggressive in making a tag at home plate.

With the bases loaded and the throw coming to the catcher from the infield for the possible double play, the catcher has the responsibility of throwing to first base after the force-out at the plate. The best method is to put the left foot on home plate for the force play, then step with the right toward the infield and extend the left foot toward first as he throws (Diagram 2-4). This footwork gets the catcher out into infield to clear the runner. This method may take a little longer, but it reduces the chance of the ball ending up in right field.

Catching the Pop Fly

Catching pop-ups at the youth-league level is not really a problem because the overhangs and backdrops are so close to the hitter. However, every coach and catcher should know that all pop-ups drift back toward the infield because of the spin imparted as the ball leaves the bat. After the catcher has located the pop-up, he tosses his mask in another direction. All catchers should face the grandstand and catch the ball as an infielder would, with the hands above the face.

Many catchers never locate the pop-up because they never see the ball leave the bat. This happens because they have shut their eyes tight at the time of contact and the ball is out of their field of vision when they open their eyes again. All catchers blink when the ball and the bat make contact, but they should open their eyes in time to see the ball leave the bat. A good method of stopping a catcher

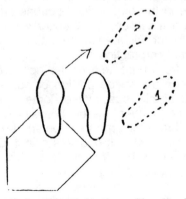

Diagram 2-4. *Footwork for the catcher in making the force play at home plate.*

from shutting his eyes at the moment of contact is to toss the ball softly into his mask so he can feel its impact. When he is sure the mask affords all the protection he needs, his confidence will improve.

The catcher should yield to pitchers and infielders who call him off pop-ups, as they have probably caught more balls of this type than he has.

General Information

In fielding bunts the catcher must use two hands (Fig. 2-16). He should hold the glove in front of the ball and scoop the ball into the glove with his bare hand. This gives him time to gain control of the ball and set up for the throw. Since he can see all the positions, he must yell out which base to throw to on bunts that he does not pick up himself.

Whenever a ground ball is hit to the infield with the bases empty or only first base occupied, the catcher must back up first base. Generally he tries to position himself so that the bag is between him and the person throwing the ball. This is hard to do sometimes especially on a throw from third base but the throw can carom off the first baseman's glove or the dugout and may bounce toward the catcher if he is hustling to back up the play.

Another common play for the catcher is to cover first base if a ball has been hit past the first baseman. The catcher trails the runner, and

Fig. 2-16. *Proper mechanics in fielding a bunt. Use both hands and keep your head over the ball while picking it up.*

the first baseman stays in short right field to tempt the runner to take a large turn at first base. The right fielder picks up the ball and throws behind the runner to the catcher covering first base. This is commonly called the "trail play."

A catcher must have a good relationship with each umpire. Never beef at an umpire's call. To have an umpire's respect, each catcher must respect the umpire and the difficult job he has to do.

Each time a runner scores, the catcher must watch to see if the runner actually touches home plate (Fig. 2-17). If the runner misses the plate an appeal play (explained in a later chapter) should follow.

Coaches should not be afraid to use left-handers as catchers. Left-handed catchers are rare because it is hard for them to stop the steal of third base with a right-handed batter up. However, good athletes at the youth-league level make fine catchers even if they are left-handed. Make sure they realize that they are only catching temporarily and that at a later time they will settle down to positions more suitable for left-handed players at the higher levels of the game. Left-handed catcher's mitts are available through local sporting-goods dealers.

Fig. 2-17. *Every catcher must watch to see if the runner touches home plate.*

The very nature of the catching position, with all the action in front of the player and with so many responsibilities, requires that the catcher be a leader. In many cases it is his attitude and influence which determine how a team will play.

A mediocre catcher can make a great pitcher look average. A great catcher can make a mediocre pitcher look great. This is true because everyone on both benches and most of the spectators are watching the catcher receive each pitch. **Remember**, your shortstop may be your best catcher.

III. The Pitcher

At any level of baseball, pitching is obviously important. At the major-league level, pitching is 85 to 95 percent of most games. The younger the players, the more important the pitchers are to the outcome of a game.

What makes a good pitcher? Can you really develop a pitcher? Is control more important than speed? Should curve balls be thrown at the youth-league level? How much rest should a pitcher have? These are some of the questions asked by concerned youth-league coaches at the start of every season. All of these questions and many more will be answered in this chapter.

There are three kinds of pitchers at the youth-league level. First, there is the youngster who has a very strong arm. He might start out as a center fielder or shortstop. If the boy is amenable, he should try pitching. He should take this step as early as possible. His coach teaches him proper mechanics, control, and other skills necessary for successful pitching.

The second kind of pitcher may have an average arm but exceptional competitive ability. This youngster has a desire to pitch and win. He is usually a fine athlete who has good anticipatory powers. A coach can help him become even better by improving his technique. Possibly he can be helped to develop another pitch or two.

The third type of youth-league pitcher comes along very infrequently. He is a boy who has always pitched, has a live arm, good size, and exceptional athletic ability. Here the coach's role is to see that the boy is not abused by being pitched too often. He should be constantly reminded about caring for his pitching arm. He should be told constantly about all the responsibilities of a pitcher so he will become a total pitcher and not just another boy with a strong arm.

Another type of player often plays the position of pitcher in youth-league contests. However, he is a thrower and not a pitcher. He usually pitches when no one else is available. He has had very little instruction, as pitching is usually his "second" position. Unfortunately, this youngster is found all too often "throwing" on youth-league diamonds everywhere.

The teaching of pitching involves showing the youngster the many fundamentals he must master to be successful at this very difficult position. These include stance, delivery, gripping the ball, various pitches, strategy, fielding, pick-off plays and conditioning. Obviously patience is necessary.

Certainly a youth-league coach cannot be expected to tutor a youngster in all the fundamentals. The short season, coupled with relatively few practice sessions and the many things a coach has to do, makes this impossible. However, if the coach picks his pitchers carefully, encourages them, and tries some of the techniques suggested, he will find coaching pitchers very gratifying.

Stance and Delivery

Stance:

In step one of the delivery the pitcher stands with his throwing foot forward and in contact with the pitching rubber. The foot should be on the right side of the rubber for a right-hander and on the left side for a left-hander. By standing this way the pitcher will create different angles of trajectory with different pitches. An inside fastball will actually be a different pitch from an outside fastball because of the difference in the angle of the path of the ball. The glove foot can be either in contact with the pitching rubber or slightly behind it. The ball should be kept in the glove and the glove should be held in front of the body and close to the chest. The pitcher should hold his body straight up. The feet are comfortably spread with the weight equally balanced on both feet (Fig. 3-1).

Fig. 3-1. *The pitcher's stance should be straight up with the ball in the glove.*

Many pitchers bend over as they look in for the signal. This position makes it harder to breathe. It also puts tension on muscles necessary to support the weight of the upper body. This position is usually a sign of a tired pitcher.

Rock:

After taking the catcher's signal, if the pitcher is using signals, he fixes his eyes on the catcher's target and begins his windup. This is step two. Most pitchers transfer the body weight by moving their left foot back (opposite for left-handed pitchers). The hands come off together in front of the body. As the hands come up and over the head the step back with the left foot is completed (Fig. 3-2). This second part is called "the rock." It is important to take only a small step back (about six inches) and to step straight back and not off to the side of the rubber.

Pivot:

In step three the pitcher pivots on his throwing foot, bringing it to the front of the rubber (Fig. 3-3). An important teaching point is to emphasize that the pitcher must not pitch from on top of the rubber.

Fig. 3-2. *The "rock" is the 2nd step.*

Fig. 3-3. *The "pivot" is Step #3. Make sure the foot is in front of the rubber.*

He will not be able to push off the rubber and get the thrust necessary for a good delivery.

He should keep his head straight up, concentrating on the target. Most pitchers get lazy at times and drop their heads during this first part of the windup.

Another major fault of young pitchers is allowing the opposition to know what pitch they are about to throw. Even in the lower division, where the pitcher is using only one pitch, he should work on hiding the ball from the opposition. This is done by wrapping the glove around the pitching hand. The ball should be held deep in the pocket of the glove. Sometimes, pitchers allow the ball to be seen when they are at the top of their windup because they forget that the fingers of the glove hand must be pointed toward the sky.

Hip action is very important in achieving a powerful delivery. While a good push-off from the rubber is essential, correct use of the hips is even more important in obtaining good velocity.

Lift:

Step four begins with the weight on the pivot foot. The hips are rotated to the right. The knee of the glove foot is brought up across the body as the arms swing down and back.

The pitcher bends his pivot leg, lowering his body and getting better position to push off the pitcher's rubber. The leg must bend to get balance and a good "explosion" off the rubber (Fig. 3-4). Pitchers who are poorly coached, lazy or in poor condition are likely to pitch with a stiff pivot leg.

Fig. 3-4. Step #4 is the "lift." The pitcher must stay straight up and be comfortable.

Stride:

Step five begins as the pitcher pushes forward, and begins the stride. (Fig. 3-5). The youngster should be reminded to uncoil like a spring. One common problem is rushing the delivery; if the pitcher is rushing, his pitches are usually high. Have him hold the ball in his glove a little longer. Rushing the delivery is one fault that major-league pitchers fight all year long.

The pitcher's glove foot should be placed almost straight forward as he steps to deliver the ball. If he steps too far to his right he will be throwing across his body. If he steps too far to his left he will not be able to get anything on the ball. Both faults can cause arm problems.

The stride should be comfortable. The length of the stride usually will depend on the pitcher's height and what is comfortable for him.

The stride should be completed before the pitcher has reached the top of his delivery. His striding foot should be firmly planted in the ground before he starts to whip his pitching arm forward. One important teaching point is that the knee of the striding leg should be flexible. A flexible front leg will allow him to obtain the follow-through he desires. Some pitchers come down very hard on the heel of the striding foot. This jarring action makes control pitching impossible. The toe and heel should touch the ground almost simultaneously, with the ball of the foot taking most of the shock. Ideally the pitcher steps in the same spot for each pitch.

The throwing arm should be away from the body. The pitcher should bring the ball down from his glove, back as far as he

Fig. 3-5. *Step #5 is the "stride," which should include the lead foot's toe pointing directly toward home plate and then the release of the ball at 10 or 11 o'clock.*

comfortably can, and forward in one continuous motion. When the arm starts forward, the wrist is bent back.

Release:

This is step six. The elbow comes through first, then the forward action of the arm and wrist. Watch to see that the pitcher's elbow is not below his shoulder and that his elbow precedes his wrist.

The pitcher must snap his wrist as he releases the ball. A strong downward snap will impart spin to the ball, which will cause the ball to "move" as it is affected by air currents. The pitcher must have a loose and relaxed hand and wrist before releasing the ball. A stiff wrist will make it impossible to throw his best pitch. To remind him, you might ask him to wiggle his hand and wrist between pitches.

The index and the middle finger pull downward on the ball to give it the spin it needs. Some smaller players will have to throw with the index, middle and fourth fingers because their hands are not large enough to hold the ball with just the thumb, index and middle fingers.

Like a bowler, the pitcher tries to create and maintain a consistent point of release. Only practice and more practice can enable a pitcher to find the correct release point. If he opens up too soon, the pitch will be high. Likewise, if he holds on to the ball too long, the pitch will probably be low and outside to a right-handed batter. This is not reaching, or failing to extend on the pitch. It is important for the pitcher to reach toward the mitt on every pitch.

The pitcher should be on top of every pitch he delivers. Remember, he should be throwing the ball on a downward plane.

Sidearm pitching causes too much wear and tear on the arm and should not be allowed at the youth-league level.

Follow-through:

A good follow-through is also important (Fig. 3-6). If the pitcher stops his motion too soon after releasing the ball, his control will be affected. His arm should snap toward the catcher's mitt and then across and down toward his left knee. His pivot foot should swing around automatically because of the push off the rubber and come to rest approximately parallel to the striding foot. He need not have a perfect finish, with his feet exactly even and facing the batter. However, when he releases the ball, his eyes should be on the target, his back bent, and his knees slightly bent. He should try to bring his glove up in front of his body to end up in a good fielding position.

A good pitching delivery seems to flow in a smooth, full arm swing, finishing with a good wrist snap and follow-through. A herky-jerky motion will cause undue strain on the arm and make it very difficult to throw strikes.

Fig. 3-6. *The "follow through." Make sure the hip and heel are used when reaching for the plate.*

A well-coordinated, rhythmic delivery will provide extra movement on the ball when it is released. Such a delivery is necessary for control as well.

There are three basic types of pitching deliveries: overhand, three-quarter and sidearm. The most common is the three-quarter method. Whichever style of delivery is used, certain fundamentals are essential. The pitcher must have balance, a proper pivot, and a good follow-through. Each pitch must be thrown with about the same motion and released from almost the same point. Only practice can give a pitcher the rhythm needed for an effective delivery.

Drills:

One effective drill that will help a pitcher gain coordination and rhythm is the "form drill." The pitcher throws the ball into the backstop or a net from only ten or twelve feet away. He concentrates on his stance, windup, pivot and follow-through. He need not throw hard. The coach must watch to see that he has his eyes on a target, that he is hiding each pitch and that he has a comfortable delivery that is overhand or three-quarter.

Another drill that is very good for any pitcher is the "chair drill." The pitcher lines his heels up with the front of the chair, about shoulder width apart. He places his pivot foot in the seat of the chair and throws to his partner or coach. As he delivers the ball he must drive his hip forward and down while rotating his pivot foot so that the sole of his shoe is facing the sky. This drill will help get the hand, hip, and foot working together.

The "one-knee drill" is good for teaching the correct arm swing. The pitcher kneels on the knee of his throwing-arm side. He brings the ball out of the glove down by his side, up and back through the backswing, and forward through the throwing motion. It is important to keep his fingers on top of the ball at all times. Twenty or thirty repetitions per day should be enough.

In throwing the ball to the bases pitchers commonly make a lot of errors. A pitcher can improve this skill by practicing the "Indian drill" and spending time in practice throwing to the bases. In this drill the pitcher sits on the ground with his legs crossed Indian style. He brings his arm back and makes a dart throw to his partner or coach. This is the proper way to throw to the bases.

These drills and many others are important for any pitcher to learn the proper mechanics. However, there is no substitute for practicing his pitches in the bullpen with his catcher and coach.

The Set or Stretch Position

When there are runners on base, the pitcher should throw from the set (or stretch) position instead of the full windup position. However, he uses the same delivery as he would from the windup. The object of the stretch position is to keep the runners close to the bases they occupy. There is no reason a pitcher can't be as effective from the stretch position as he is from the windup. If you have a pitcher who just doesn't seem to throw well with men on base, chances are that he never practices pitching from a stretch. He probably never practices a pick-off move either. He must gain confidence and work at this important phase of pitching. Some of the most important pitches in every game will be delivered with runners on base. It makes sense to practice pitching from a stretch in anticipation of the rough innings.

Some youth-leagues prohibit the base runner from leading off until the ball reaches the batter. But these leagues usually have standard rules for baserunning at their higher levels. So I think it would be wise to include information about holding base runners on.

The stretch motion begins by placing the outside of the pivot foot against the front of the pitching rubber. The body is facing third base for right-handers (first base for left-handers), and the shoulders bisect the pitching rubber vertically. Once again, the pitcher should stand straight up and not hunch over when taking a signal from the catcher. The throwing arm is held comfortably against the chest. The front foot takes a small jab step back toward the pivot foot as the hands come together. The hands should come to rest somewhere near the waist (Fig. 3-7). A common mistake made by pitchers is that they reach their set position with their hands below their waist. While this is legal, it takes too long to throw the ball to home plate, thus allowing a base runner time to steal a base (Fig. 3-8).

From the set position, the pitcher can throw to any base, step back off the rubber or deliver the ball to home plate. In order to hold the runner close to first, the pitcher must have some type of pick-off move to first base. No signal is necessary. The pitcher should pivot quickly on his right foot, take a short step with his left foot toward first base and deliver a throw there.

Even a pitcher, without a fine move to first, can work on holding the runner there. He should vary the amount of time between each pitch. For example, when he reaches the set position, he can count to three and then throw home. The next time he only counts to one and throws home. The next time he counts to four before he delivers the ball to home plate. The base runner will not be able to get a good

Fig. 3-7. *Here the pitcher is in a good set position. He can vary the amount of time between each pitch by holding the ball a different length of time; he can throw to first; he can back off the rubber and start again.*

Fig. 3-8. *Here the pitcher has a poor set position. His hands are too loose; they should be above the belt. His shoulder is opened up too much. It will take him too long to pitch the ball to home plate, giving the runner time to steal.*

jump because he obviously will not know when the ball is going to be thrown home.

Left-handed throwers have an advantage in holding runners close to first base. They should be able to learn a move to first in which it appears as if they are throwing the ball toward home. This is legal as long as their right foot does not cross the front edge of the rubber. If it does, they must throw the ball to home plate. A left-handed pitcher should be able to practice looking home and throwing to first while playing catch every day. Soon he will find that runners will leave first as soon as he lifts his front leg. He can then throw to first base, finding that his ability to pick off base runners at first base will grow as he continues to practice his move to first.

With a runner on second base, the pitcher must once again reach a set position and pause for about a second before delivering the ball to home plate. There are two important coaching points regarding holding a runner close to second base: first, make sure the pitcher looks to second more than one time. Don't allow him to be a "one-looker" enabling the runner to steal as soon as the pitcher turns his head. Have him look once, twice and even three times before he throws home. Second, when the pitcher wants to throw to second base for one of the pick-off plays described in later chapters, he should pivot to his left. This move also requires practice. The shortstop, second baseman and pitcher can come up with signals and pick-off plays of their own if they are given the opportunity. Of course, pick-off plays in the lower divisions are very rare.

With a runner on third, the pitcher can stretch or use a full windup. A stretch might be more beneficial if the squeeze play is a possibility. A right-handed pitcher can develop a pick-off move to third, very similar to the left-hander's move to first. It is very effective, but because the situation comes up so infrequently, most right-handers and their coaches are reluctant to use it.

Regardless of where the runners are, the coach must be aware of one major flaw of youth-league pitchers. They fail to pick up the target before they deliver the ball to home plate. For example, if a pitcher is holding a runner on first from the set position, before he decides to pitch the ball he must pick up the catcher's target. Not doing this will cause control problems.

All pitchers should be aware that they do not have to complete their throws to either second or third, but that they must in throwing to first base. If a pick-off play at second base is impossible because there is no one covering the base, the pitcher does not have to complete his throw even though he has pivoted. The same is true at third. However, any move to first base must be followed by a throw to the bag or a balk should be called.

The Pitcher as a Fielder

The pitcher is "the fifth infielder" when he is not in contact with the rubber, and his ability to handle ground balls and bunts and to throw well to the bases makes the difference in many games. Covering first base and backing up bases are also important responsibilities of the pitcher.

After the follow-through the pitcher must be ready to field any ball he can reach. He must attempt to catch all ground balls. There are no balls that belong only to the third or first basemen. If the pitcher can reach them, they are his. The pitcher should not be excluded on pop flies either. Usually he is one of the best athletes on the field. If he is close to the pop fly, he should call for it and catch it.

On bunt plays the pitcher must break for home plate as soon as he has released the pitch. As he nears the ball he must get under control and slow down. He must field it with two hands, rise to a throwing position, point the toes of his striding foot toward the base he wants to throw to, and deliver a hard throw.

Good judgment is needed by the pitcher in fielding bunts. If another player calls for the ball, the pitcher yields. If the ball appears to be rolling foul, he allows it to roll across the foul line and then picks it up immediately so it will not roll back into fair territory. If he feels a bunt is on, he should throw a fastball high in the strike zone. This pitch is usually popped up by inexperienced bunters.

On any ball hit to the pitcher's left, he automatically breaks toward first base. If the first baseman fields the ball, he throws to the pitcher covering the base. If the ball is hit directly to the first baseman or a little to his left, the pitcher runs to a spot about ten or twelve feet in front of the base and approaches it running parallel to the foul line. As he approaches the base, he slows down and gets under control so he can catch the ball and tag the base too. Hopefully, he will get the ball a full stride or two in front of the base.

Another method of covering first base may be used on a ball hit to the first baseman's right. Sometimes the second baseman fields the ball. Possibly he will fumble it. In any event, the first baseman runs directly to the base and anchors himself there. He might also stay there on a double-play attempt in which the first baseman throws to the shortstop and the shortstop returns the throw to first base. On occasion, because the diamond is smaller, the second baseman can cover first on this play.

With a runner on third and a wild pitch or passed ball, the pitcher must cover home plate and take the throw from the catcher. Actually, any time the catcher leaves home plate, the pitcher should be ready to cover.

The pitcher should run in as fast as possible, drop down on his right knee, and face the intended throw. He should stop just short of the plate, giving the runner the outside portion of the plate. He does not want to block the plate, because of the possibility of injury. When he receives the ball, he places it down in front of the plate with the back of his glove facing him and lets the runner tag himself out by sliding into the glove.

Every ball hit to the outfield is a potential backup play for the pitcher. It doesn't matter which base the runner starts from or how many runners are on base. The pitcher should get about forty feet behind the base to which the ball is likely to be thrown, if he is not sure which base to back up, he takes a position between the bases until the outfielder makes his throw.

Because of the small diamonds lower-division players use and because of the short distances on regulation youth-league diamonds, it is possible to use the pitcher as the cutoff man instead of having him back up a base. Sometimes this is a good idea because of the reasons mentioned in the introduction and because of the athletic skill of the pitcher.

Control and the Various Pitches

If the most important ingredient for successful pitching had to be singled out, it would be control. Control makes the difference between a winning pitcher and a losing one. This is especially true at the youth-league level. Many youth-league teams do not have enough good hitters to produce runs against a pitcher who won't walk anyone. A team needs at least two hits, sometimes three (excluding home runs), to produce a run without the aid of walks or errors. A pitcher without control not only provides walks but may also promote errors; many youngsters playing defense lose their ability to concentrate after a lot of balls have been thrown.

Many pitchers also do not concentrate enough. Often you will see a pitcher throw three balls in a row, then throw two strikes because he knows he must or the batter will walk. This is simply concentration. A pitcher must not wait until he is behind in the count to start throwing strikes. He must start off each batter by "thinking the ball over the plate." Let him carry a home plate with him once for an entire practice session.

Control pitching in this discussion means throwing strikes anywhere in the strike zone. While low strikes, strikes with breaking pitches or strikes on the outside corner are preferable, most youth-league coaches will be happy with a pitcher who can throw a strike when he needs one.

Good control takes practice. A pitcher should throw to his catcher and count the number of strikes he can throw out of every ten pitches. The pitcher must check the grip of the ball, his delivery, and of course his release point.

After making sure that your pitchers have practiced control pitching on the sideline, here are some points you will want to remind them about:

1. Get ahead of the hitter. Try to get that first pitch in for a strike.
2. Never take your eyes off the catcher's target. (If a pitcher does not keep his eyes on the target, use an eye patch to help him. The patch, which can be bought in any drugstore, should be placed on his left eye [right if he is a left-hander]. This will force him to turn and face the target so he can see it with his other eye.)
3. Do not start to pitch until you are sure that you are ready.
4. Always pick up the target before throwing home when pitching from a stretch.
5. Don't rush your motion. (If it appears that the pitcher is doing this, have him hold the ball in his glove as long as possible during his windup.)

The basic pitches are the fastball, the curve ball and the change-of-pace. There will be no reference here to pitches such as the screwball, knuckleball, forkball, palmball, slider, slip pitch, sinker, or splitfinger fastball. While these pitches and others actually do work for many professional pitchers, **they should not be experimented with by youth-leaguers.**

For the fastball, the pitcher will grip the ball in a manner that is most comfortable for him. The successful grip is the one in which he gets the most out of the pitch. You may suggest that your pitchers try various grips and let them decide which one is the best. At the lower levels, however, you should have your pitchers hold the ball across the seams (Fig. 3-9).

The fastball is still the king of all pitches. It also has a strengthening effect on the arm. Youth-league pitchers should rely on it almost exclusively. It is not only the best pitch for strengthening the arm but the pitch least likely to cause injury.

One of the greatest concerns of parents and coaches is that pitchers may develop painful inflammations of a shoulder or elbow. Two kinds of injury have become common. One is epiphysitis, an inflammation at the still-growing ends of bones. The other is osteochondritis, an inflammation and fragmentation of cartilage. Many have called these conditions "Little League Elbow." The term is unfair, I believe, because these injuries occur often in unorganized sandlot games and in other sports as well.

The danger of epiphysitis is that a boy's elbow may not bother him

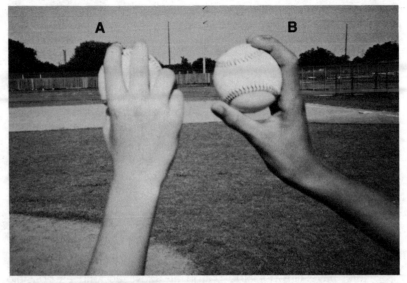

Fig. 3-9. Holding the ball across the seams as shown in both A and B is a good grip for beginning pitchers when throwing a fast ball. Don't let them grip the ball too tightly. If possible, leave space between the ball and the palm of the hand.

enough for him to complain until he's finished the season. The symptoms may develop gradually over a period of several seasons. The best prevention against injury to a pitcher's arm is a concerned coach. The first sign of pain in the shoulder or elbow should be enough to get the youngster medical attention. Certainly no youngster should pitch with pain in those areas. However, the large muscle groups of the arm may be sore, and they usually are, after pitching. Pain in the forearm, back, or biceps is usually the result of not being prepared to pitch and over using these muscles. Usually, rest will take care of this soreness.

Continuous hard throwing or improper throwing can cause arm problems. "Trick" pitches, sidearm throws, or too many curve balls at a young age can be dangerous. League rules should prohibit lower-division pitchers from pitching more than six innings a week. Older boys may go up to ten innings a week.

A key factor for a coach is to see whether or not his pitcher labors when he throws. If he throws with a smooth, easy motion as he pitches, then chances are he will not have arm problems. If he labors—that is, if he has to work very hard because he is not as fluid as he could be—then check him frequently to see if his arm is sound..

Fortunately most youth-league coaches and leaders are very concerned about the problem of arm care. Pitching rules protect most youngsters from being over pitched. However, these rules do not include penalties for pitching sidearm or in many cases for throwing curve balls. The rules also do not affect practice sessions or unorganized games. Here is where the coach must impress upon each youngster the importance of arm care. He can use his influence and knowledge to help prevent an unnecessary arm injury. The rule book itself is not enough.

The curve ball has been blamed for most of the arm injuries in youth-league baseball. Most orthopedic surgeons agree that throwing curves puts an unusual strain on a boy's throwing arm. Most would agree that curve balls should not be thrown by boys under fourteen. Some leagues prohibit the curve ball in games for boys under twelve or even under fourteen, which I think is a good idea. However, the curve ball will still be used by boys in other leagues and in sandlot games. For this reason I feel it is necessary to mention the proper mechanics in throwing the curve ball.

Years ago the curve ball, when thrown overhand, was referred to as a "drop." A curve ball properly thrown should break mostly down. Even in a three-quarter delivery a well-thrown curve breaks down and over. So the term "drop" is out; all curves should spin so that the rotation takes the ball down. Flat curves, thrown sidearm, or with a three-quarter delivery, should be discouraged.

The pressure of a gas (like air) decreases as the speed of the gas increases. A baseball in flight will move in the direction of the least air pressure. This is why the rotation of the ball, or spin, is so important. The faster the spin, the less the air pressure in the direction of the spin, thus the better the ball's movement.

The best grip for the curve ball is shown in Figures 3-10 and 3-11. The elbow is above the shoulder. This is very important. The elbow starts forward first, and the wrist turns over and snaps downward to impart a downward spin to the ball, which is released over the first and second joints of the first finger.

The longer the pitcher can hold on to the ball, the better the curve he will throw. He must be on top of the ball and put pressure on with his middle finger. As his throwing arm comes down, he must pull down hard, snapping his wrist as the ball is released over his index finger.

Most pitchers can learn to throw the curve ball. To practice getting the correct spin a youngster can have another player stand ten to twenty feet away and just spin the ball into his glove. Results may not come overnight. However, any player with a supple wrist can learn to throw a curve ball properly.

Very few youth-leaguers can hit a good curve. Even professional pitchers have indicated that very few major-league batters can hit the curve ball consistently. But an improperly thrown curve ball can

Fig. 3-10. *The front view of the curve ball grip. Hold the ball with the seams, on the narrowest part, where they come together. The ball should not be gripped tightly.*

Fig. 3-11. *The rear view of the curve ball grip. The elbow is up and the wrist is twisted so the palm of the hand is facing the head. A hard wrist-snap is necessary as the ball is released over the index finger.*

cause arm problems and youngsters who throw too many curves can injure their arms over several seasons. A concerned coach will watch to see that his pitcher throws the curve ball properly. He will also see that his pitcher does not overuse his curve ball, regardless of his success with the pitch.

Without a good change-up, a pitcher is limiting his effectiveness. Youngsters in the upper division can learn to throw an off-speed pitch or change-up very easily. The pitch puts no extra strain on the arm. A change-up, even an average one, gives the batter another pitch to worry about.

The grip for the change-up should be the same as the one for the fastball. The ball is held a little further back in the hand (Fig. 3-12). It is also held slightly looser. The pitcher delivers it by pulling down, rather than whipping his throwing arm across his body as he would in throwing a fastball. The movement is similar to pulling down a window shade. The wrist is stiff and does not snap downward as in the fastball release. The heel of the hand comes down first.

The motion for the change-up should be the same as that of the fastball. Otherwise the batter will know the pitch is coming. Make sure you don't speed up your preliminary motion in an effort to fool the batter; this also tips him off that a change-up is coming. A three-finger grip is easier for some boys and can help reduce wrist snap.

Fig. 3-12. *The change-up can be a very effective pitch. It's fun to work with and puts no extra strain on the arm.*

A good change-up takes a great deal of practice. A pitcher can practice his change-up while warming up on the side with any player. He need not use a catcher. The thing to watch is if the pitcher is slowing up the arm action as he starts to release the ball. Remind him that he can whip his arm as long as he does not snap his wrist. He can drag his right foot, which I have found to be very helpful for young pitchers learning this pitch. As they throw the change-up, they try to leave their right foot on the pitching rubber. This cuts down on the speed of the pitch.

Don't be alarmed if the first few attempts at the change-up go over the catcher's head. Practice often and the change-up can be mastered. Remember, changing up simply means taking some of the velocity off the ball. Change-ups can be thrown at medium, slow, and even slower speeds. They're fun to work with and they can be very effective.

General Information

A pitchout is a deliberate ball that is usually thrown high and outside. The batter is not supposed to be able to hit it. Its purpose is to let the catcher throw to one of the bases. The pitchout should be used when you think the other team will steal, hit-and-run, or try a squeeze play.

Many youth-league pitchers, trying to rush the pitchout to the plate, throw the ball very poorly. If the catcher has to reach too far to catch it, the pitchout is wasted. It should be a shoulder-high fastball.

Another strategic technique is the intentional pass. In giving an intentional pass the pitcher should not bloop the ball up to the plate but should throw medium-speed fastballs, shoulder-high. The catcher should be prepared to step out and catch the pitches.

The intentional pass is in order only if first base is open. Usually in youth-league baseball it is saved for a few exceptional hitters.

One of the mistakes youngsters make is not warming up enough before the game. The first inning is when most runs are scored, because the pitcher usually is not warmed up and the opposition has its best hitters up. Special care must be taken to make sure your pitcher warms up for a long enough time. Usually fifteen minutes is long enough. On an exceptionally hot day, the time can be reduced, and possibly on a very cool night it can be increased. Regardless of the time, the pitcher should start with his fastball, include all his pitches, and throw at least one-third of the time from the stretch position. He should work very hard warming up and finish about five minutes before he is going to take the pitcher's mound for the game.

Often in youth-leagues the pitcher does not bat ninth. Even if he will bat before he pitches, he should finish warming up about five to ten minutes before he comes to bat. If you expect to use another pitcher who is starting the game at another position, let him warm up before the game also.

Many pitchers can attribute some of their failures to the fact that they are not in proper physical condition. Pitchers, even young ones, should run sprints in the outfield so their legs will always hold up when they are pitching. More and more pitchers are taking part in strength-building programs using weights. This is a very good idea if the program is supervised by a knowledgeable coach who has had much experience in this area.

A method of strength development that many youngsters can take part in is isometric exercise. Pitting one muscle against the other can build strength and increase body tone. The most common isometric exercise for increasing arm strength is demonstrated in Figure 3-13. The youngster should push hard against a doorway or on the side of a dugout or batting cage for six seconds.

Fig. 3-13. *Isometric exercises are easy to do and are beneficial. Here a youngster increases arm strength by holding this position and pushing against an immovable object for 6 seconds.*

Calisthenics have considerable value in maintaining flexibility and as a warm-up activity. Another key to any conditioning program for pitchers or any other players is stretching. The back muscles and other muscles necessary for throwing are loosened up by hanging from the top of the dugout or from a doorway or a bar (Fig. 3-14). This is usually done for fifteen to thirty seconds each day.

Because of the strain put on a pitcher's arm during a ball game, he needs a period of rest before he can pitch again. In normal seven-inning games a pitcher will throw approximately ninety pitches. If he throws ninety pitches on Monday, he should throw softly to a catcher for ten minutes and run sprints on Tuesday. On Wednesday, he should throw softly to a catcher for ten minutes and run his sprints again. On Thursday, he should throw, even batting practice, and run his sprints. On Friday, he should rest, with no throwing, but he can go through an ordinary practice session. He should be able to pitch another game on Saturday.

If the pitcher works harder, say throwing 110 pitches, then he might wait until the following week to pitch. The coach and his pitchers can be the best judges of when to pitch and when to rest. Remember, any

Fig. 3-14. Hanging from a bar or dugout before throwing loosens up the back and other muscles necessary for throwing. Hang for 15 to 30 seconds.

pain in the shoulder or elbow means he must not pitch; he should receive medical attention.

A pitcher's clothing should be loose. Most pitchers use cotton undershirts with the sleeves cut just below the elbow. The pitcher must have a jacket or heavy sweatshirt to wear when he is finished pitching. He must not let the breeze or cool air hit his throwing arm when it is not in use. Encourage your pitchers to bring an extra jacket to each practice and to get into the habit of using it after they pitch.

A pitcher's proper mental attitude is very important to the team's overall performance. He must display confidence and poise. Because of the importance of the position, a pitcher with a strong competitive spirit can help his team before it ever takes the field. He must appear to have everything under control to be able to dominate the game.

The pitcher must show courage and not be afraid to throw the ball over the plate. He must be aggressive when fielding balls and throwing to the bases. A competitive pitcher, one who takes charge, makes a coach's job much easier.

IV. The First Baseman

Playing first base calls for more variety of talent than most of the other positions. Fielding bunts, communicating with the other infielders working in cutoff situations and handling low throws in the dirt are normal plays for the first baseman. Nothing can instill greater confidence in the infield of a team than a first baseman who scoops balls out of the dirt for an out.

The youngster selected to play first base need not be tall or left-handed. The advantage of a left-handed first baseman is that he can throw to second base for the double play without having to pivot as a right-handed first baseman would. This advantage is only applicable in professional baseball. There are far too few double plays to even consider the throwing hand in selecting a youth-league first baseman. A sure pair of hands and the ability to stop most balls are better criteria. A good-fielding first baseman will win many more games than a hard-hitting first baseman who is placed at first with the idea that anyone can play there.

The first baseman is the only player allowed to use the special mitt which is longer than the rest of the fielder's gloves. This type of mitt allows the ball to be caught in the webbing. He may also use a regular fielder's glove, especially in the lower division.

Getting to the Bag

The first baseman should be at least six feet off the base and six feet back from the bag when there is no runner on first. When a ground ball is hit, he must get to the bag as quickly as possible and set up. There are two methods for awaiting a throw from an infielder. The first method for upper-division players and for highly skilled lower-division players is to heel the base (Fig. 4-1). The heels are in contact with the base before the ball is thrown so that the player knows exactly where the base is at all times. He faces the appropriate infielder and awaits the throw. He gives no target on a normal infield play. He waits with his knees slightly bent so he can shift either way by sliding his feet on the edge of the base to keep the ball in front of him. He tags the base with the ball of the foot at the very edge of the base (Fig. 4-2). Do not allow him to tag with his foot on top of the base or he may be stepped on.

Fig. 4-1. Heeling the base for the skilled first baseman.

The second method of awaiting a throw is to place the ball of the left foot in contact with the edge of the base. Again the knees are slightly bent (Fig. 4-3). The ball of the right foot may be used if this is more comfortable. In either case, the youngster must learn to anticipate a poor throw rather than set up for a perfect one.

The most common fault of young first basemen is that they commit themselves too soon. If the play appears to be close, they stretch out too quickly and the ball passes them by. They must learn to wait, then shift and, if necessary, stretch.

Fig. 4-2. Proper tag using the ball of the foot.

Fig. 4-3. *Using the one-foot method while awaiting the throw.*

One of the biggest plays in baseball is the first baseman's stretch. In many cases it's the difference between the runner being out or safe. The stretch makes the two-handed catch impossible. Most balls, however, can and should be caught with both hands. Have your first baseman try to get his head behind his mitt so that he can follow the flight of the ball into the mitt.

The throw into the runner is possibly the toughest for a first baseman to catch. He will have to tag the runner if he feels that he cannot stay on the base. Only practice can determine on which play he can stay in contact with the base and on which play he must leave the base and tag the runner or stop the ball from going through.

Low balls are extremely tough. The first baseman must stay low and keep his eye on the ball (Fig. 4-4). He must give a little with his hands and not get caught standing up or turning his head. This scoop can become routine if the youngster will practice handling low throws. The "stretch and scoop" drill is absolutely necessary for every first baseman. To make sure the first baseman receives low throws, and all other types of throws that he would get in a regular game, the coach stands forty-five to sixty feet away and throws baseballs at him (Fig. 4-5). The first baseman should have a base to practice making the tag correctly on each reception. Someone to back up the first baseman is necessary if a backstop is not available. The coach will throw high balls, balls to the inside and outside and bouncing balls. Soft rubber baseballs may be used for this drill, and they are strongly recommended in the lower division.

Fig. 4-4. *Good position while reaching for a low throw.*

Fig. 4-5. *The "stretch and scoop" drill is a must for every first baseman; soft rubber balls may be used for this drill.*

Another type of tag that a first baseman must learn is the "inside-outside target" (Diagram 4-1). For example, when a catcher drops the third strike and the ball rolls in foul territory to the first-base side, an outside target is necessary. When a ball is bunted directly in front of home plate and does not roll too far for the catcher to field, an outside

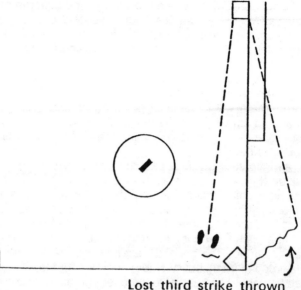

Lost third strike thrown
on foul side of first base

Diagram 4-1. Correct trajectory of the throw for the "inside-outside target."

target should be used. For an outside target, the first baseman stands with the right side of his right foot in contact with the base. His left foot is slightly in back of his right foot and his feet are about shoulder width apart. He holds the target chest high and directly at the catcher or fielder who is throwing. He shouts "Outside, outside" so that the fielder will know the situation. To give an inside target he places the side of his left foot on the inside part of the base, right foot slightly back, and the feet shoulder width apart. He holds the target chest high and directly at the player who fields the ball. Again he should communicate, shouting "Inside, inside."

The inside-outside target will prove useful on balls that must be fielded in foul territory or are just inside the foul line on the first-base side.

Fielding Ground Balls

The first baseman must think of himself as an all-around fielder. He must leave first base to field ground balls and line drives hit into his territory. The youth-league first baseman will mistakenly go directly to the base on most balls hit unless he is taught which balls he can handle and which belong to the second baseman or pitcher. The only way to accomplish this is for the coach to fungo balls to the first baseman's right and between the first baseman and pitcher until the youngster realizes which are his. **Communication must be stressed.** A strong shout, "I got the ball," responded to by "I got the bag," will help. Usually the best idea is to have the player who feels he can get the ball shout "I got it," rather than have someone assume that a teammate will be able to get it and shout "You take it." All players should converge on the ball until one is sure that **HE** has the ball. Only after someone calls "I got it" may his teammates shout his name or "You take it."

Like all infielders the first baseman must assume a position of anticipation (Fig. 4-6). He keeps his glove low as the other infielders do. However, a first baseman may drop to one knee and block a ground ball where other infielders cannot. Upon recovering and getting to his feet, if he cannot beat the runner to the base he should throw to the pitcher, who is covering the base. Sometimes on small baseball diamonds the second baseman can take a throw to first from the first baseman, but it is more common for the pitcher to take it because he should be parallel to the base runner and no collision will follow his tag of the base. The throw to the pitcher should be made with the arm stiff and thrown underhand (Fig. 4-7). Give the ball to the pitcher as soon as possible so he will not have to look for the base and the ball at the same time. Once a first baseman commits himself on a ball to his right he keeps on going even if he cannot get to the

Fig. 4-6. *Like all infielders, the first baseman must assume a position of anticipation before each pitch.*

Fig. 4-7. *Good form on the throw to the pitcher covering first base. Get the ball to him as soon as possible.*

ball. The second baseman can field the ball and throw to the pitcher covering.

A good pitcher will start toward first on every ball hit to the left of the mound, so the first baseman must wave him off when he can make an unassisted putout. Don't wave him off with the hand that the ball is in. The ball can be dropped accidentally. Shout to him, "I've got the bag," and motion him away from the bag with the hand that is free. Sometimes a play becomes so close that the first baseman and baserunner approach first at the same time. To avoid a collision, the first baseman should use a straight-in slide and touch the base with his foot.

Handling Bunts

When a first baseman fields a bunt he should always assume he will make the play at second base. Otherwise, it may be too late. If a bunt situation is likely, the first baseman moves toward the batter and looks at his bat; when the bat is dropped into position to bunt, the first baseman can charge the hitter. He should always tell the second baseman beforehand that he is going in so the second baseman will cover first.

Many coaches have the catcher call the bunt play. That is, the catcher tells the first baseman where to throw the ball. However, a first baseman must think who the runners are before fielding the ball, and most of all how hard the ball was bunted and whether it was right to him or off to a side. How smoothly the first baseman fields the ball is also a factor. While the catcher must help, each first baseman must rise up and throw overhand. He must point his toe in the direction he wants to throw the ball.

Holding the Runner On

All players must be in fair territory when the ball is pitched. The first baseman must have both feet in fair territory when holding a runner on. While the pitcher is in his stretch position the first baseman sets up (Fig. 4-8). Most players have their right foot to the side of the bag, with their left foot just before the foul line. The first baseman faces the pitcher, his body slightly crouched, and extends his mitt as a target.

He should be ready to handle any throw from the pitcher. No signal need be given. It is the responsibility of the first baseman to constantly watch the pitcher and be ready for a throw any time. To tag the runner, the first baseman must go directly for the edge of the bag and not for the runner's foot or hand. The runner should tag himself out by sliding or diving into the first baseman's mitt. Hold the tag there because the runner may slip off the base (Fig. 4-9).

Fig. 4-8. *Be in good position to catch a throw to either side when holding a runner on first base.*

Fig. 4-9. *Go directly to the edge of the base when making a tag. Do not go for the baserunner's hand or foot.*

With men on both second and first, there is no need for the first baseman to hold his runner on. He can play behind the runner and receive a throw from the catcher or pitcher, but here a signal must be given. The first baseman may rub his chest or touch his cap to indicate he is going to the bag before the pitch if he wants the pitcher to throw, or after the pitch if the pick-off signal is for the catcher.

Catching Pop Flies

The first baseman should call for and take any pop fly to the right side, if he can move in and make the catch. However, the cardinal sin in fielding pop flies is calling them too soon. Wait until the ball reaches the apex of its flight. When the ball is called for too soon, the flight of the ball may later indicate that another infielder would have an easier catch. All infielders, pitchers included, should converge on pop flies. When one is sure of the catch he hollers "Mine" or "I've got it," and all of the other fielders call out his name. In youth-league baseball many youngsters will not call for the ball. Nothing is worse for team morale than to have a seemingly harmless pop fly drop in and the runner reach base. At the lower levels a team captain can be used, the pitcher or shortstop, for example. He will not catch all the balls, but he will decide who will. Be careful that the captain does not call out someone's name too early. The captain may think someone is able to catch the ball when that person is not too sure. Make sure that the captain knows his teammates well and that he will wait long enough for the ball to start coming down before calling out who should take it. Collisions happen in big-league baseball not because the players will not call for the ball but because they both call for it at the last second.

I feel that priorities as to who should catch the ball at various parts of the diamond are not necessary in youth-league. The pitcher, catcher, shortstop or whoever is certain he can catch the ball should take it.

On pop flies that are near the fence or dugout, the first baseman must go to the barrier first, then look for the ball. This is better than running while looking up at the ball and feeling your way to the fence or dugout, which can end in a collision. When chasing a pop fly, get to the fence as soon as possible.

Cutoff and Relay Position

At most levels of baseball the first baseman lines up between the right fielder and the catcher, becoming the cutoff man for throws to home plate. He also does this for the center fielder. When acting as a cutoff man, the first baseman must line up the throw to home plate as accurately as possible by having the catcher yell "Left" or "Right." The first baseman stands as tall as possible with his arms extended in order to make a good target for the outfielder to throw to (Fig. 4-10).

The position taken by the first baseman depends on the strength of the throwing arm of the outfielder. The stronger the arm, the closer to home plate; the weaker the arm, the closer to the outfielder. The purpose of the cutoff man is twofold: first, to help the outfielder in his throw; second, and most important, to cut off the ball if there is no chance of getting the runner at home plate. Sometimes the cutoff man can catch the ball and throw the ball home. The first rule for the cutoff man is to catch the ball if it does not come directly to him. Obviously, if the throw does not accurately reach the cutoff man it will not accurately reach the catcher. The catcher will yell "Cut home" if he feels that there is still a chance of getting the runner. He should yell "Cut second" if there is no chance of getting the runner at home but the first baseman can cut the throw and get a runner going to second base.

At all levels of baseball infielders should go back toward the outfield on a pop fly and keep going until they hear an outfielder call them off by yelling an unmistakable "I got it." The outfielder should have an easier chance coming in than the infielder going out.

Fig. 4-10. *The cut-off man must line up the throw and, if it is poor, prevent the runner from taking another base.*

Similarly, pop flies behind first and third are easier for the infielders who are playing deeper to begin with—the second baseman and shortstop—than for the first and third basemen.

Good throws to cutoff men are about shoulder-high, and if let go they reach the catcher on one bounce. Throws too high are obviously not good even if they reach the catcher without a bounce, because the cutoff man has no chance of catching them.

In the lower division, and even the upper division, don't be afraid to use the pitcher as a cutoff man on all throws to home. While this is not acceptable at higher levels of the game, it is perfectly good baseball at the youth level. The reasons are that the fields are very small, and the normal role of the pitcher, to back up home plate, is unnecessary if the distance behind home plate to the backstop is very short. Secondly, the pitchers are usually the best athletes and therefore will be better at handling the throw. Of course, the very young players cannot be expected to throw the ball directly to the cutoff man. Their number one priority is to throw the ball to the correct base. They can only accomplish this if teammates and coaches yell to them as they are picking the ball up.

A good cutoff man always fakes catching the ball when he does let it go through. This is to fool the batter-runner into thinking he is cutting the throw off and making a throw to get him. Hopefully the runner will stay at first base.

Another teaching point for a first baseman and any cutoff man is that he should catch the ball with his body turned slightly toward the base he intends to throw to. He can maneuver into this position as the ball is in flight from the outfield.

General Information

When the bases are unoccupied, the first baseman backs up second on all throws from the left side. For example, after a single to left he should be ready to retrieve overthrows to second base. He also covers second base if the second baseman and shortstop go out for a pop fly in short center field. The first baseman should back up the pitcher covering home plate if a runner tries to score from third on a passed ball and he should back up the pitcher during a pick-off at third.

The first baseman should yell "There he goes" or "Going" when a runner is stealing from first base. This is particularly helpful with a left-handed batter partially impairing the vision of the catcher.

The good first baseman needs practice catching pop flies, grounders and all kinds of throws to first base as well as throwing to other bases, mastering the rundown play (covered in a later chapter), and handling bunts.

A first baseman should always watch to make sure that a base runner touches first base after a hit, especially an extra-base hit. He should stand on the infield side of the base and out of the baseline, being careful not to interfere with the runner, and watch to see that he touches the base. If the runner misses the base, then he should call for an appeal play (covered in a later chapter). It takes much practice to condition your first baseman to watch runners tag the base. Telling him is simply not enough; he must develop the habit.

Certainly first base is a position for a youngster who is alert and courageous and one who loves to play.

V. The Third Baseman

Playing third base demands sharp reflexes, quick thinking, a good pair of hands, and an accurate arm. Running speed is not essential, but quick reactions and movements are requisites of successful third-base play.

The difficulty of the position is compounded by the necessity for fielding bunts and slow rollers. Handling bunts and dribblers requires the ability to throw from any position. Hard-hit balls can often be blocked instead of fielded cleanly, but the third baseman needs agility to retrieve the ball and make a play on the base runner.

Third base is often called the "hot corner." In youth-league baseball, however, the third baseman will not have to worry as much about hard smashes as he will slow rollers and bunts. The inability of lower-level right-handed hitters to pull the ball hard down the left field line makes the label of "hot corner" a misnomer in the youth leagues. Because of the consistent activity at third, however, and the number of times a third baseman will handle the ball, this is a position for a good athlete. At the major-league level there has been a tendency to place the weakest infielder at third base. For the above reasons, however, the weakest infielder should be at second base rather than third.

An aggressive, competitive athlete is needed at third base—one who is willing to dive after balls (Fig. 5-1) and stay in front of hard-hit

Fig. 5-1. *The third baseman must be willing to dive after many balls and block many others with his body.*

and tough-to-field balls. Quickness is more important than speed and the ability to throw accurately is more important than an exceptionally strong arm.

The Glove

An infielder's glove can be his best friend. Most third basemen, as well as other infielders, prefer a glove that is shorter than those outfielders use. The glove must be used often in order to be broken in properly. Glove oil and leather conditioners can be applied, but only constant use will make the glove feel comfortable. Infielders should not catch the ball in the webbing of the glove. An infielder's glove should not have a deep pocket like an outfielder's because infielders have to get rid of the ball quickly.

The stance, like that of other infielders, is a semi-crouch. The feet are spread shoulder-width apart. The knees are slightly bent and the glove is down (Fig. 5-2). The infielder's back should be low enough so that it is almost parallel to the ground. The left foot is slightly ahead of the right foot. The third baseman, like all players, should expect every ball to be hit to him. If he does, he will be ready to make the play.

Positioning and Fielding Ground Balls

The fielding position of the third baseman depends on a number of factors. He must consider whether the batter is a pull hitter or a late

Fig. 5-2. *The third baseman moves a half step forward as the pitcher releases the ball. He is then in the position of anticipation, or ready position.*

swinger. Does he bunt often? Does he run fast? These are questions a third baseman must ask himself.

Normal position is three or four steps from the foul line. The depth ranges from about even with the base to two or three steps beyond the base. If the pitcher is pitching with good velocity, chances are that the hitters will not hit the ball with authority to the third baseman. If this is the case, he may play a step closer to the batter and a step closer to the shortstop.

Bunt position or double-play depth means the third baseman plays two or three steps in toward the batter. If the ball is hit it will reach him sooner and he will have a chance for a double play. If the batter lowers his bat as if to bunt, the third baseman charges in to field the bunt.

A third position, used only late in the game, is called the deep position. Here, the third baseman wants to protect against an extra-base hit. He plays three or four steps beyond the base and only one step from the foul line. If the ball passes him on his left it will only be a single. At the same time he will be able to prevent any ball from getting by him on his right for a double or more. This position should be used in the late innings, particularly in a tie game or when protecting a one-run lead.

Regardless of his position, the third baseman always takes every ball he can reach. Youth-league players make the mistake of thinking that some balls belong to the shortstop and others to the third baseman. The third baseman should try for every ball hit to his left. If he finds that he can't reach it, he should continue on to give the shortstop an opportunity to catch it.

An infielder must stay as low as possible when fielding a ground ball. It is easier to come up for a high hop than to come down for a ball that stays along the grass. To some extent the third baseman can pick his own hop if he plays the ball and does not allow himself to become a slave to the batted ball. He must try to catch each ball at the maximum height of its bounce (Fig. 5-3). The four pictures in Figure 5-3 indicate that the third baseman may charge some balls to get a good hop or wait back on other balls to avoid getting an "in between" hop.

The ball should usually be fielded with two hands. The fielder has time to get the proper grip on the ball if he uses both hands to bring the ball into throwing position. The weight comes back on his right leg, which braces and pushes the body forward.

Most third basemen rate the slow roller as the toughest ball to field. This is the unexpected hit that comes as the result of a topped ball or bunt. The only time a youngster should employ the one-hand technique, as shown in Figure 5-4, is when the ball is rolling slowly or has stopped. The infielder should not make the barehand play as in

Fig. 5-3. (Series of four photos)

A,B,C, & D. The third baseman must work to get a good bounce. Judgment determines whether he will charge the ball or wait for a good bounce. The coach must hit different types of balls to the third baseman so that he can find the best way to play each ball. In [A] the third baseman has an excellent hop. In [B] the hop is good. In [C] the hop is only fair, and [D] illustrates that an in-between hop means trouble.

Fig. 5-4. *This is the correct way to pick up a rolling (not bouncing) ball or a ball that has stopped. Note the fingers coming up from beneath the ball.*

Fig. 5-5. *This is the wrong way to attempt to pick up a ball that has stopped or is rolling. The fingers are pointed down.*

Figure 5-5, or he'll have a tough time trying to grip the ball and throw it to first base. If the one-handed technique is used, the third baseman must have his eyes squarely on the ball. He should not worry which foot comes down next to the ball. The fingers must pick it up from beneath as if using a shovel. The leg bends to get the body low to the ground. The player comes up throwing off either leg, whichever comes naturally.

If the ball is bouncing or rolling fast, two hands should always be used and the ball should be fielded between the legs. A better grip is obtained by pushing the ball into the glove with the throwing hand while getting into throwing position.

A ball hit right at the third baseman can be a tough play. If the third baseman stays low and in front of the ball, however, he can still get the runner at first even if he does not field the ball cleanly.

The coach should show the third baseman just how far down the baseline a runner can get on a ball hit directly at him. The coach can do this by standing in the batter's box and hitting a hard ground ball right at the third baseman. After the coach has hit the ball, he moves to first as a batter-runner would, but he stops as soon as the third baseman catches the ball. The third baseman will quickly note the short distance the coach has traveled, and should indicate that he has plenty of time to get any runner if the ball is hit directly to him. If he does not field the ball cleanly, he still has time to pick it up and make the play at first base. If he fields it cleanly, he should take his time, stepping directly toward first base, possibly even taking an extra step or two. Remember: "Knock it down. Don't let it get past you."

In making a double play always follow the old saying, "Get one for sure." The third baseman must give the pivot man the ball quickly, about letter-high over the base. He picks up the ball, braces on his right foot, and uses the three-quarter throwing method.

When the bases are loaded, the third baseman has several ways to make a double play. If he fields the ball near enough to third, he should step on the base and then relay the ball to second or first. But if there are none out and the situation calls for a double play from home to first, he should throw home; the catcher should relay the ball to first for the second out. The coach must help out in this situation. Because a double play is unlikely at the lower levels of youth baseball, the coach may want to tell the third baseman what to do with the ball before it is hit. This way, no reaction on the part of the youngster will be needed. For example, with runners on first and second and one out, the coach may tell the third baseman, "If it's hit to you, just step on third for the force."

Bunt Situations

With a runner on first and the sacrifice on, the third baseman must move in, two or three steps from his normal position. His first reaction to the bunt will be made easier if he "reads the bat," or watches the thick end of the bat in the batter's hands. If the bat is lowered, he charges. If the bat remains still, he holds his position. If the ball is bunted to him, he listens to his teammates, particularly the catcher, tell him which base to throw to. An upper-division player may be able to throw to the right base by judging just how hard the ball was bunted. If it reaches him quickly, he will have a chance to get the runner at second. If the ball is tough to get, or if he bobbles it, the play will go to first base.

If the third baseman fields the bunt, the catcher must cover third base to prevent the runner from going all the way from first to third. The shortstop should cover second base and the second baseman should cover first. The first baseman should be charging the bunt. If the pitcher or first baseman fields the ball, the third baseman must get back to third base himself.

One of the toughest plays for a third baseman is the bunt situation with a runner on second or runners on first and second. On this play the third baseman is still up for the bunt, but he cannot charge it unless he is sure that the pitcher can't get it. He must decide whether to move in to field the ball or return to the base and let the pitcher play the ball. Ideally, of course, the pitcher will play the ball and throw it to him for a force-out.

The first teaching point in this situation is that the third baseman should remind the pitcher to cover the left side. Don't let your third baseman commit himself too soon. The pitcher is aware that he must cover the left side. After the pitch he should break toward the foul line a step or two in anticipation of a bunt in that area. The third baseman will break for the bag if he's sure that the pitcher can get the ball. If not, he'll field it himself and throw to first base.

Another defensive variation of the play, which can be used in the upper division, is to have the second baseman break for second before the pitch, while the first baseman holds at first and the shortstop breaks for third and covers it. This leaves the third baseman free to charge the bunt and possibly throw to the shortstop for a tag or force-out at third.

Another bunt situation is the squeeze bunt. The batter attempts to bunt any pitch to get the runner home from third base. The third baseman's job is to yell "Squeeze" if the runner leaves when the pitcher is in his windup. He then charges the plate and attempts to return a bunted ball. If there is no play at the plate, he must throw to first base. The shortstop should break over to third and cover there in case the batter misses the ball and the runner is caught between third and home.

Tags and Cutoffs

On all tag plays the third baseman should straddle the bag. The ball should be in his glove and immediately in front of the base (Fig. 5-6). He faces second base with his feet on either side of the base, an inch or so behind the front edge. He looks for the runner's foot and allows the runner to tag himself out by sliding into the glove. Many youth-leaguers make the mistake of reaching out to tag the runner. Invariably the umpire calls the runner safe, claiming that he slid under the tag. The glove must be brought down quickly and aggressively to indicate to the umpire that the player making the tag has everything under control. Tags must be practiced. The coach has to line up all the infielders, throw the ball to them, and watch to see if they are quick and aggressive. He must see that they position themselves correctly with feet straddling the base and the glove placed so that a runner would have to touch the glove in order to reach the base. Some players can use both hands when making a tag if this is comfortable for them. Most players, however, will tag with one hand

Fig. 5-6. *Good position for a tag-out. The runner should slide into the glove and tag himself out.*

and immediately lift their glove up as the sliding base runner tags himself out.

On base hits to left field, the third baseman acts as the cutoff man for the throw to home plate. His position is in a direct line from the left fielder to the catcher and between the pitcher's rubber and the foul line (Fig. 5-7). He listens for the catcher to tell him whether to cut the ball off and throw to second base to stop the batter-runner from getting there, or to let the throw go and try to catch the runner from second at the plate. If he feels the throw won't reach the catcher without his help, he moves into position to receive the throw from the left fielder and relays the ball to the catcher.

The shortstop covers third base when the third baseman acts as cutoff man. On throws to third from the outfield, shortstop is the cutoff man. The third baseman should assist him by yelling "Left, left!" or, if necessary, "Right, right!" He yells "Cut, third," if he thinks the throw won't reach him without the help of the cutoff man. If the throw appears to be good he says nothing or, if the coach prefers, "Let it come" (Fig. 5-8).

General Information

On throws from right field, the third baseman backs up second base unless there is a possible play at third. He also backs up the

Fig. 5-7. *The third baseman acts as cutoff man on a single to left field with a runner on second base. He should make a good target to align the throw from the left fielder to the catcher.*

Fig. 5-8. *The third baseman aligns the shortstop who acts as cutoff man for throws to third base.*

pitcher on throws from the first baseman after a pick-off attempt at first.

The third baseman should take most pop flies between third and home plate. He should call for any ball he can reach and is sure he can handle. On fly balls to the back of the infield he runs back until he hears the shortstop or left fielder call him off the ball by yelling "Mine," or "I got it." On foul fly balls near the fence or dugout he should follow the technique described for the first baseman. He should move to the fence as quickly as possible, then locate the ball and move back to the spot where it will come down.

With a runner on third and a right-hander pitching from the stretch position it is possible for a pick-off play to work. The third baseman gives the pitcher a signal and starts to the base as the pitcher starts to pitch. The pitcher makes a deceptive move, appearing to get ready to pitch home while he actually throws to third. He looks toward home plate but steps toward third base.

A more common pick-off play with a runner on third involves the catcher and the third baseman. The third baseman signals the catcher before the pitch. After the pitch is received he moves to third to receive the throw from the catcher. Before this play, the third baseman should signal the left fielder that a pick-off play is about to happen. After the pitch, the left fielder hustles over to back up the play in case of a poor throw.

Each day the third baseman must spend time fielding ground balls of all types. He must especially work on bunts and slow rollers. The "slow roller drill" is the perfect solution for helping the third baseman play this difficult ball (Fig. 5-9). Line up three baseballs about four yards apart in front of the third baseman, who is playing at normal depth. Have him charge the first ball, pick it up with both hands and throw to first, then charge the second ball immediately. Again he makes a two-handed play and throws to first. However, when he charges the third ball, have him try a one-handed pickup and throw to first.

Naturally, the first baseman must be aware of the drill in order to be ready for each throw. Doing this drill four times will enable a third baseman to practice the play a dozen times. Later, the coach can roll or fungo the balls to the third baseman one at a time.

Fig. 5-9. *A good drill for all third basemen is the "slow roller drill." The third baseman should work this drill every day. Other infielders would also benefit from this drill.*

VI. The Second Baseman

Second base is a very challenging position. The youngster who plays it must be alert and intelligent. He must be prepared to handle many different types of ground balls, cover first base on bunts, and take part in various pick-off plays. At the professional level one of the most important qualifications of a second-base candidate is the ability to make a double play. The youth-leaguer, however, will take part in too few double plays to worry about this very difficult skill. Instead, the youth-league second baseman should have a sound knowledge of the game because of the many decisions he must make during the game.

Catching the Ball

"Keep your eye on the ball!" or "Watch the ball into your glove!" are phrases that cannot be spoken too often. All players should catch the ball with two hands whenever possible. As stated before, this places the throwing hand on the ball as it hits into the glove. Many youngsters catch the ball with only their glove hands. Then they have to reach into the glove with their bare hand to gain control of the ball. If a youngster catches the ball with both hands, he'll not only make a surer catch but also move more quickly into throwing position.

The youngster must keep his hands relaxed. He must wait for the ball to come to him instead of stretching to reach the ball and tightening his arms. He has to give with the catch. This will become automatic with practice.

Catching the ball is simply a matter of practice. During warm-up, make sure the players take their time and pay attention (especially in the lower division). Each youngster should watch the ball come out of his throwing partner's hand and into his own glove. When returning the ball, the youngster should pick out some part of his throwing partner's body, such as a knee or shoulder, and aim for that part. This improves throwing accuracy.

Should a player continue to catch the ball with one hand after being continually told not to, the coach shuld have him use the "wooden glove." The "wooden glove" (Fig. 6-1) is fastened to the player's hand with an elastic band stapled to the wood. This is not a commercial item, but a coach can easily make it himself. The

Fig. 6-1. A "wooden glove" should be used by the youngster who is trying to break the habit of catching the ball with one hand.

youngsters really enjoy it, and they benefit from it as well. If a "wooden glove" is not available, have the player use a very rigid catcher's mitt. In either case, the habit of catching the ball with one hand will soon be broken.

Stance and Basic Fielding Position

The second baseman takes a stance similar to that of other infielders once the pitcher has released the ball. The feet are about shoulder-width apart and the weight is evenly distributed on both feet. The glove is close to the ground. On each pitch, the second baseman steps forward about six inches with his left foot, then makes a slight shuffle with his right foot. Being in motion at the time of the pitch allows players to use Newton's first law, "A body in motion tends to remain in motion; a body at rest tends to remain at rest."

With no one on base, the second baseman plays deep. His exact depth depends on the hitter, his own throwing ability and, in many cases, how well his pitcher is pitching. If it appears that his pitcher is throwing very fast, he moves to his left, anticipating a late swing. The condition of the playing field is also a factor.

With a runner on first, the second baseman must move into double-play depth. He moves two or three steps closer to second base and two or three steps closer to home plate. This movement is not so much for the double play itself as it is for the covering of second base on a steal attempt and getting the lead runner on a ground ball.

If the second baseman is going to cover first base in the event of a bunt, he must move three or four steps toward first before the pitch. He tells the shortstop he is going to cover first, and the shortstop covers second on a steal, bunt, or ground ball.

Fielding Ground Balls

The second baseman has the advantage of a shorter throw to first when he picks up a ground ball. He also has more time than the third baseman on ground balls as he is farther from home plate. However, he will field many types of ground balls.

As he fields the ball, his tail is down and his knees are bent. He must stay in front of the ball with his head down. He must not lift his head. A good expression for the coach to use to make sure the head is down is, "Let me see the back of your neck!"

More often, it is better to charge ground balls than to stay back or back up. One of the worst habits that infielders develop is trying to be too certain of getting the good hop. They lose their aggressiveness and find themselves letting the ball play them.

One of the hardest plays for a second baseman is the ball hit directly at him. This play can be tough because he does not have a chance to gauge the hop of the ball. On a hard-hit ball, the second baseman tries to knock it down and still throw the man out (Fig. 6-2).

A slow roller is also a very difficult play. It is best to field the ball with the left foot forward. Pick it up with two hands, take a step with

Fig. 6-2. A second baseman can't be afraid to get his uniform dirty. He must dive after and knock down many balls because he can get up and still throw the runner out at first base. Never give up on a ground ball.

the right foot, and then make the throw. Only if the ball has stopped or is rolling very slowly should it be picked up with the bare hand; in this situation the out usually cannot be made any other way.

Another difficult play is the ball hit to the second baseman's right. This play must be practiced often. The second baseman pivots on his right foot and crosses over with his left foot. If he can, he gets in front of the ball instead of fielding with a backhand stab at it. He then braces his weight on his right foot and turns to make the throw. Once again, the throw should be overhand or three-quarter rather than sidearm.

Making the Double Play

The secret in youth baseball isn't in making the double play, but in getting one out for sure. Too many youngsters, inspired by television announcers and coaches at the higher levels of the game, rush to make the double play and end up with not even one out. While the double play is the pitcher's best friend, youth-leaguers must work to get one out at a time.

The second baseman gets in position by moving over and in for double-play depth. If a ground ball is hit, he must get to the bag and take the position shown in Figure 6-3. From this position he can

Fig. 6-3. *Proper position while waiting for the throw from the third baseman or shortstop. Upon receiving the throw, the second baseman will move toward the pitcher's rubber, then step to first with his left foot while completing the throw.*

reach the throw to his left or right by properly shifting his feet. Don't allow the second baseman to make the mistake of committing himself too soon. He waits until he sees the throw, then moves toward the throw to give the runner room to slide. He receives the ball with both hands if possible. He shuffles toward the pitcher's rubber and points the toes of his left foot toward first base as he throws to complete the double play.

If the ball is bobbled, or it appears that the play will be very close, the second baseman must take a first baseman's stretch (Fig. 6-4). He knows there will be no chance of getting the runner at first so he makes certain he gets the one at second by stretching for the ball.

When a ground ball is hit to the second baseman in a double-play situation, he must angle field it as shown in Figure 6-5. He turns his

Fig. 6-4. *The proper stretch position is necessary when the play will be very close at second and no throw to first base will follow.*

Fig. 6-5. *The second baseman must angle-field a ground ball to avoid a very difficult pivot for the throw to the shortstop.*

body slightly toward second base before fielding the ball so that he can avoid a pivot before throwing to the bag. The pivot is time-consuming and more important, it does not allow the second baseman to get set and give the shortstop a fine throw. A good throw is just below the left shoulder. Don't have your players throw the ball too hard. Remember, "Get one out for sure!"

If the ground ball to the second baseman finds him close to his base, he can give the ball to the shortstop with an underhand toss. He brings his glove into his chest, keeps his throwing elbow stiff, and tosses the ball in a straight line without blooping it (Fig. 6-6).

If the second baseman is very close to the base, he'll try to tag it himself. He must communicate his intentions to the shortstop. He may also tag a runner and throw to first base as well.

Another reason for playing close to second is to be ready for a throw from the catcher to prevent a stolen base. When the runner breaks from first, the second baseman holds his ground until the ball passes the batter. This permits him to field a ball hit his way. If the ball is not hit he goes to the base and straddles it before the catcher's throw comes. He can get there if he has cheated over a few steps closer to second in anticipation of the steal. He should take the position shown in Figure 6-7. After catching the ball he tags the runner the same way other infielders do, aggressively placing the glove and ball down in front of the base to let the runner slide into it and tag himself out.

Fig. 6-6. *When the second baseman is close enough, he should use an underhand toss to give the ball to the shortstop.*

Fig. 6-7. *Proper position for waiting for the catcher's throw when covering second base on a steal attempt.*

The Double Cutoff

When the ball is hit between the outfielders and it appears that the batter-runner will have at least a sure double, the double cutoff should be used. Both the second baseman and the shortstop go out to receive the throw from the outfield. The one who has the stronger arm (let us assume this is the shortstop) goes out to a position in the outfield where he feels the outfielder can reach him with a relay throw. The second baseman stands four or five yards behind the shortstop. If the relay throw comes directly to the shortstop, the second baseman tells him where to throw the ball. If the ball is over-thrown, the second baseman fields it and relays it to the infield. This gives a team added protection against a poor throw from an outfielder. The first baseman trails behind the base runner so that he can cover second in case the runner takes too large a turn past it but decides to return rather than going on to third (Fig. 6-8).

The only other cutoff position for the second baseman would be to line up a throw to second base in the event of a single to right field or right center field.

Many outfielders in the lower division find this cutoff procedure difficult. They must be told time and time again to hit the cutoff man rather than throw all the way to the base or into the infield.

Fig. 6-8. *Here is the double cutoff with the shortstop and second baseman going out for the relay throw. The first baseman trails the runner and covers second base.*

Rundowns

When a base runner is caught between bases, he is in what is referred to as a "hot-box" or "pickle." He should be caught almost every time. At the youth-league level, however, the runner seems to escape more often than not. If your defense will follow a few rules and is willing to practice, your team will get almost all the runners.

To practice the rundown drill have all the outfielders wear helmets and act as base runners. Place all the infielders, pitchers and catchers behind second and third. Line up all the outfielders about two-thirds down the baseline toward third. Throw the ball to an infielder at third base and have him start the rundown.

The first rule is to run the base runner back to the base he started from. The teaching point here is: the infielder must run at top speed to get the base runner to commit himself. The infielder should hold the ball high, and his arm should be still. Do not allow him to fake continually with his throwing arm. If he is in the process of faking when the runner breaks, he'll have to rush his throw. The infielder waiting to receive the throw should be two steps in front of the base and on the throwing-hand side of the player who has the ball. If the thrower is right-handed the receiver will be on the left side of the base. If the thrower is a left-hander, the receiver will be on the right side of the base. This avoids throwing over the runner.

The cardinal sin in rundown procedure is **holding the ball too long.** When an infielder has run at top speed, and has forced the runner to run at top speed also, he can no longer afford to hold the ball. He should give a soft throw to his teammate waiting at the base and then follow his throw. This means **he does not back up** and receive another throw should the base runner return. He takes the place of the player to whom he threw the ball. An ideal rundown would have only one throw. This would not allow time for other base runners to advance. Also, the fewer throws, the fewer chances of making an error (Fig. 6-9).

General Information

With a runner on third base, the second baseman and/or the shortstop should back up the pitcher every time the catcher returns the ball after a pitch.

The second baseman also has the responsibility of backing up first base on throws from the third baseman or shortstop. This applies only if there were no baserunners before the pitch.

The second baseman must practice constantly with the shortstop. They must play catch, throw to each other, and work together on

Fig. 6-9. *Rundown procedure involves running the baserunner back to the base he started from, if possible. One throw, or two at most, is all that is necessary in any rundown. The cardinal sin is holding the ball too long. Always follow the throw; never back up after throwing the ball.*

possible double plays. He must spend each session picking up at least twenty-five ground balls. These include the hard smashes, slow rollers, and balls hit to his right and to his left.

Practice sessions must include various situations such as covering first on bunts, catching pop flies and acting as the cutoff man.

Whenever possible he must watch to see if base runners touch second base on their way to third. If they should miss the base, an appeal play would follow. The appeal play procedure is explained in the next chapter.

During warm-up, the second baseman should keep moving back until he is throwing the distance he would throw from his deepest area behind second base.

If two runners end up on second base at the same time and the second baseman receives the ball, he should tag both runners and yell, "You're out! You're out!" Actually, only the second runner is out, but possibly both runners will step off the base. Then the second runner to reach the base can be tagged out (Fig. 6-10).

The second baseman need not be your best athlete. However, he must have confidence in himself. He must hope that every ball will be hit to him.

If an infielder should pick up a ball and throw it away, the coach can still commend him for picking up the ball. Nobody can be expected to make all the plays. The infielder and coach should forget the error, think of the positive things accomplished, and make sure he grabs up the next ball and plays it perfectly.

Fig. 6-10. *If two runners end up on a base at the same time, tag them both and shout, "You're out!" Actually, only the second runner is out, but possibly both runners will step off the base.*

VII. The Shortstop

The shortstop is the key man in the infield. Very few teams can win a championship without an outstanding shortstop. The shortstop must be able to throw out runners after backhanding a ball in the hole toward third base. He must have the speed to reach ground balls behind second and the agility to throw accurately after picking balls up. The shortstop will handle more balls than the second and third basemen combined.

Not only does he need speed and quickness to reach ground balls, but it is essential that he field the ball cleanly. Unlike the second and third basemen, with their shorter throws, the shortstop cannot afford to fumble a ground ball. In addition to fielding ground balls and making double plays, the shortstop must also cover second base on the steal and handle pop flies. He must handle cutoffs and cover on bunts and pick-off attempts. Therefore, the shortstop must be the type of youngster who is resourceful and who has a talent for anticipating plays.

The shortstop is most often the type of athlete who is the team leader. He must be a "take charge" type of player, and the one who will keep his teammates on their toes. Other than the pitcher, youth-league shortstops are the most important defensive players.

Stance and Basic Fielding Position

The basic fielding positions for the shortstop depend largely on his own ability and the type of hitter at the plate. On a regulation diamond the shortstop will play about thirty feet from second base. On a diamond that has bases sixty feet apart, the shortstop will play about twenty feet from second base. He is anywhere from ten to fifteen feet behind the baseline on a small field and twenty to twenty-five feet behind the baseline on a regulation playing field.

With a right-handed pull hitter the shortstop plays more toward third base. With a left-handed hitter he plays more toward second base. However, don't let your shortstop move over until you're sure which way the batter is likely to hit the ball. Do not assume that just because the batter is hitting left-handed he will hit the ball to right field. Far too many youth-leaguers hit the ball to the opposite field because they swing at the pitch a little too late. Yet I see shortstops and outfielders automatically start moving to their left because a left-handed batter steps up to the plate. If you don't know the hitter, then play him straight away until you watch him swing at a few pitches. The shortstop should move in for fast runners whether they bat right- or left-handed.

With a runner on first, the shortstop should move into his double-play depth. This is about three or four steps toward the batter and two or three steps toward second base. He should be able to cover second base on a bunt or steal. He must also be in position to receive the throw for a double play.

With a runner on second base, no one out, and a bunt situation in order, the shortstop moves directly behind the base runner. This will leave his fielding position vulnerable, but he must hold the runner as close as possible. He does not need to stand on second base until the pitcher releases the ball. Pick-off plays will be discussed later in this chapter.

The stance for the shortstop is the same as for other infielders. He must take a short step with his left foot followed by another short step with his right foot as the pitcher throws the ball to the batter. This allows him to have some movement as the ball is pitched so he will not be flat-footed. His knees are bent and his glove is touching the ground. He should learn to do this before each pitch (Fig. 7-1).

The shortstop and third baseman in Figure 7-2 show how most youth-leaguers get into the "ready position." If a player leaves his hands on his knees, he will take more time to get to the ball. In addition, he is likely to be on his heels when the ball is hit, rather than the balls of his feet as he should be.

Fig. 7-1. *The shortstop and third baseman show good form for the ready position before each pitch.*

Fig. 7-2. *Here the shortstop and third baseman show poor form as they wait for the ball to be hit. The players should be on the balls of their feet, and the hands should not be on the knees.*

Fielding Ground Balls

Every infielder must stay low on ground balls. He should be in front of the ball. He should keep his glove close to the ground, because it is easier to come up on a ball by moving the hands up than by bringing the whole body down. The ball should be fielded with both hands.

A common mistake of many infielders is fielding the ball too far underneath them as in Figure 7-3. When they do this their gloves are usually too high because they are not bending enough. Make sure the shortstop and all infielders field the ball out in front of their bodies so they may follow it into their gloves with both eyes (Fig. 7-4).

The shortstop will move in on almost all ground balls hit his way. A slow bouncing ball hit just past the pitcher will require a quick off-balance throw. This is the same as the slow roller hit to the third baseman. If the ball has stopped or is rolling slowly, it may be picked up with the bare hand. Otherwise both hands should be used.

If the ball is hit to either side of the shortstop he must cover ground quickly by using the cross-over step. The cross-over step must be used on the toughest play of all for the shortstop, the ball hit to his right (Fig. 7-5). Since he is a great distance from first base, he must get control of his body very quickly, straighten up, and make the long throw to first base. He must plant his right foot, sliding it in the dirt and fielding the ball at the same time. He should always get in front of the ball if he can, but if he cannot, this difficult backhand play is necessary.

Fig. 7-3. *Here the shortstop has let the ball get too far underneath him. He will not be able to get low enough to field the ball cleanly and set for a good throw.*

Fig. 7-4. *Here the shortstop is in good position to field the ball. As the ball approaches, he has his glove close to the ground and his bare hand next to the glove. His elbows and hands are away from his body.*

Fig. 7-5. *Good form using the crossover step on a ball hit to the shortstop's right. He should only backhand balls that can't be reached any other way.*

When the ball is hit to the shortstop's left he must once again use the cross-over step. He pivots quickly on his left foot and crosses over by taking a long step with his right foot (Fig. 7-6). Once again, he should try to get in front of the ball. If he cannot, he must keep his glove low to the ground and "give" a little as the ball enters his glove. He then must rise up and wait to throw until he turns toward first. He should point the toes of his left foot toward first base before throwing there.

Fig. 7-6. *Good form using the crossover step on a ball hit to the shortstop's left. He must "give" a little with his hand and arm just as the ball reaches the glove.*

Making the Double Play

As I have mentioned before, few double plays are turned over at the youth-league level. This very difficult skill cannot be mastered by most youngsters until they reach the upper division, and even then only the exceptional athletes ever learn the skill. The coach's main teaching point must be to get his shortstop into position to get one out for sure. If the double play can be made, then that's a bonus.

The double-play pivot is easier for the shortstop than the second baseman because he comes to the bag moving toward first base, while the second baseman is almost always moving away from first base.

The most important teaching point is to have the shortstop ready at second base to accept the second baseman's throw. He should not be running when the throw is made. He must be able to adjust and receive a poor throw and still get a force-out at second base.

To get to the base on time the shortstop must "cheat" over before the pitch. He must move into double-play depth, shorten up and move closer to the bag.

As soon as the ball is hit, the shortstop, if he is responsible for covering second base, will try to get to the base as quickly as possible. Most shortstops run hard until they get a step or two from the base. Then they stop just a little to the center-field side of the base. They have their weight evenly distributed so they can move to either side for the throw.

After receiving the throw, the shortstop usually uses the drag method in attempting to complete the double play. He drags his foot across the back corner of the bag and gets into position to make his throw to first base. Most professional shortstops angle off between first base and the outfield, keeping away from the sliding base runner.

All baserunners should be taught to slide into base when a double-play situation exists. The main reason is to avoid being hit by the return throw to first base. A secondary reason, at the upper levels of baseball, is to break up the double play by sliding close to the infielder who is making the play at second base. Youth-league ballplayers should never consider trying to slide into the shortstop or second baseman with the intention of hurting him. It is the responsibility of the base runner to avoid being hit by the ball and the job of the infielder making the pivot at second to avoid the sliding runner.

Communication

The shortstop usually gives the sign to the second baseman as to who will cover the base on a steal or double-play ball. He usually does this by hiding his face from the opponents with his glove and giving the "open" or "closed" mouth sign (Figures 7-7 and 7-8). The open mouth means the second baseman will cover, while a closed mouth means the shortstop will cover. Another common method of communicating with the second baseman is to have the shortstop cross his letters or his belt with his right hand, meaning "You take it!" or "I take it!"

Whoever has decided to cover second also has the responsibility of holding the runner close to the base before each pitch. To do this effectively, the shortstop, second baseman and pitcher must have a few pick-off plays. Even if the pick-off plays do not catch the runner off second base, they will show him that if he gets too far off, the defense is capable of getting him out.

The shortstop must signal the pitcher whether or not he wants a pick-off play before the next pitch. Taking the glove off the left hand and holding it in the right, and touching the cap, belt, or shoe are good signals. After the signal, the shortstop waits until the pitcher has reached his set position (ball and glove are held still just about the pitcher's belt). The shortstop then breaks directly for second base and the pitcher turns his head toward home plate, counts "one thousand one," pivots, and throws to the base. The second baseman

Fig. 7-7. *Here the shortstop is giving the second baseman the "open mouth" signal, which means the second baseman should cover the base.*

Fig. 7-8. *Here the shortstop gives the second baseman the "closed mouth" signal, meaning that he will cover the base on an attempted steal.*

should have exactly the same play with the pitcher if he is the one who is going to hold the runner close. The direction in which the batter is most likely to hit the ball is the key factor as to who is going to cover second or hold a runner on. If the batter appears more likely to hit to the right side of the diamond, the shortstop will cover. The second baseman can then move farther from the base and cover more ground.

Another common pick-off that can be executed at the youth-league level (upper division) uses both the shortstop and second baseman. It is for the runner who goes back to the base when the shortstop fakes, but then takes a long series of shuffles after the shortstop goes back to his position. The shortstop gives the signal, waits for the pitcher to reach the set position, and breaks for second base, but goes only a few steps and retreats to his normal position. When he begins retreating, the pitcher turns his head toward home plate and the second baseman breaks for the base. The pitcher counts "one thousand one" and throws to the second baseman at the base.

These plays are referred to as "count plays." Make sure your pitcher doesn't start counting until he turns his head toward home plate.

There are many pick-off plays at second base. The important coaching point is for the players to understand that success is not proved by how many runners you pick off but how close they stay to second base. Of course you must practice pick-off plays if they are to be successful.

The Appeal Play

Whenever possible the shortstop must watch to see that the base-runners have touched second or third. Should he or any other infielder feel a base was missed, an appeal play must follow before the next pitch. If a baserunner tags up after a fly ball but someone in the infield feels he left the base before the ball was caught, an appeal play is also required. In either case, the closest infielder to the base should call for the ball and tag that base. In doing so the infielder should "appeal" to the umpire saying, "He missed the base" or "He left too soon."

What seems to make the play confusing is that time must not be out. If time was called, then the pitcher must put the ball back into play by taking his stretch position, going to his set position, and pausing. He then steps off the rubber and throws to the infielder, who makes the appeal. Remember, no appeal play can take place after the pitcher throws another pitch or after a team leaves the infield.

General Information

The shortstop follows the same procedures as other infielders in catching pop flies. He goes back into the outfield until he hears an outfielder call him off the ball. He can also be expected to catch balls behind third base that are too deep for the third baseman. In many cases, your shortstop makes the best "captain" of the infield. Other than the pitcher, he is usually the best athlete in the infield.

The shortstop must take part in the double cutoff explained in Chapter 5. He must also act as cutoff man on all throws to third base from the outfield. In doing so he must line up directly between the outfielder and the third baseman. He usually stands about forty-five feet in front of the third baseman, depending upon who is throwing the ball and how large the playing field is. He must be close enough to the outfielder to catch the ball on the fly. He must stand tall, extend his arms and call for the ball (Fig. 7-9). If the throw appears to be off target, he automatically cuts it off and either throws to third or stops the runner who hit the ball from getting to second base. The shortstop should also act as cutoff man on a single to left field with no runners on base.

The shortstop covers second base on all bunt plays and most ground balls. He must cover third base when the third baseman is the cutoff man. He must cover second base if the first baseman is the cutoff man.

Fig. 7-9. The shortstop acts as the cutoff man on all throws to third base that come from outfielders. He also acts as cutoff man on a single to left field with no runners on base and the throw going to second base.

The shortstop should back up second base if the second baseman is covering for the steal. He should also back up third base on throws from the catcher.

The shortstop should be such a good competitor that even if he makes an error on a ground ball he thinks about getting a runner at another base. This situation could come about with a runner at second base and a ground ball hit to the shortstop's right. He misses the ball but keeps it in front of him. The runner moves from second to third, the shortstop fakes a throw to first and attempts to get the runner rounding third base (Fig. 7-10).

All infielders must remember not to quit after booting a ground ball. Bluff a throw and look for another runner rounding a base.

The shortstop must practice the double-steal defense. He must work out a defense with the second baseman when there are runners on first and third. He must work against all possible bunt situations. He must work on his pick-off plays.

Naturally he must take many ground balls and throw to first base as much as possible. A really great drill the shortstop and second baseman can work together is called the "short hop" drill. When warming up, the shortstop and second baseman get about fifteen

Fig. 7-10. *Never stop, even after missing a ground ball. Fake a throw to first and look for another runner rounding a base. In this case the shortstop has no chance for the runner going to first, but he might get this runner rounding third.*

feet apart and slowly back up to thirty feet or more. They should be on their knees (Fig. 7-11). The purpose of the drill is to learn how to handle the tough in-between hops that are thrown by their partners. This drill also strengthens the arm and improves throwing accuracy.

The shortstop must not forget rundown plays and footwork for the double play. He needs work on pop flies and tagging runners.

Of all the youngsters on the field, the shortstop must be among the top in athletic skill. He should be the one youngster you have who is coachable and has the respect of teammates.

Fig. 7-11. *The "short hop" drill, usually done with the second baseman, improves the ability to catch the ball on the in-between hop. This drill also improves throwing accuracy and strengthens the arm.*

VIII. The Outfielder

At any level of baseball we often find that outfielders are the most neglected group of players on the field. Coaches invariably place a youngster in the outfield because he can hit, but they fail to prepare him to cope with the many defensive situations he will be confronted with. It is true that an outfielder may play a full game or two and never field a ball. However, an error in the outfield is usually a triple or a home run. It is doubtful that a slow-moving youngster who can hit the ball will drive in more runs than he'll let in by playing poorly in the outfield.

Outfielders are faced with problems like the sun, the wind, bad lights, poor backgrounds and in too many cases a lack of understanding about how to handle the position both mentally and physically. As a coach you must know your outfield is an important part of your defense and should not be neglected.

The prime requisites for a competent outfielder are speed and the ability to throw the ball accurately. The qualifications for the various outfield positions differ somewhat, and the following guidelines should be observed whenever possible.

The left fielder will handle many tough chances like curving line drives, hard-hit singles, and deep fly balls. He should be the second fastest of the three outfielders. A right-handed player has an advantage because he can field a single down the line and release the ball to second base faster than a left-hander. The outfielder with the weakest arm should be in left field. He must throw the ball home like the other outfielders, but he has a shorter throw to third base.

The center fielder should be the top outfielder because he will handle more balls than the others. He has more territory to cover and he may have to back up the right and left fielders as well. He must have speed and the overall athletic ability to judge many different types of fly balls. He must have an aggressive attitude toward defensive play. While a powerful arm is not necessary, an accurate arm is a must. Your center fielder must be your best all-around outfielder.

The right fielder who is left-handed has an advantage covering against a ball hit down the right field line and releasing a throw to second or third. He does not have to pivot as a right-hander does. The right fielder must have a strong throwing arm. He not only has to throw to home plate, but he has a difficult throw trying to stop a base runner going from first to third. At the youth-league level, the right fielder will field many balls. However, the fly balls will not be as difficult as those hit to center field and left field. Not many left-handed batters can pull the ball very hard, and, not many right-handed batters hit with authority to the opposite field.

Stance and Basic Positioning

The outfielder should use a comfortable stance, one that enables him to go in any direction with the quickest movement. He should be in a semi-crouch, with his right foot slightly back. His hands should not be on his knees; they should be held out in front of the body. The glove is not held low to the ground as in the infielder's ready position. The outfielder should step up with his left foot and follow that with a short step with the right foot as the pitcher releases the ball. The outfielder does not want to be on his heels when the ball is hit. He should be on the ball of each foot (Fig. 8-1).

After gaining confidence, the outfielder will soon learn to relax. This is important in obtaining quick starts.

Playing the hitters is extremely important. In youth-league baseball the coach must move his players around, or chances are they'll stay in the same place for every hitter. There is no reason that the outfielders have to be an equal distance apart from each other. If the center fielder is the strongest of the three, then he should shade over

Fig. 8-1. *The outfielder's ready stance is similar to that of the infielder. The glove need not be as low as the infielder's, but the ready position is necessary.*

a step or two nearer the slowest outfielder. If the center fielder has great speed and ability, then the other outfielders could move closer to the foul lines.

Outfielders must always check the wind before every inning. This is usually done by throwing up blades of grass. The outfielders should always position themselves a step or two in the direction of the wind.

Outfielders usually play too deep, resting against the fence if there is one. Many times they play too deep because they lack confidence in going back after a fly ball. If the hitter is known to be very good, or if he is very big, then backing up a step or two might be wise. It is also reasonable to back up a step or two if the pitcher has fallen behind the hitter 2-0 or 3-1; more long balls are hit with the pitcher behind in the count. If there is a runner on second or third, then a step or two toward the batter is in order in case a throw to the plate is necessary. If the infielder in front of the outfielder has great speed and can go back for a pop fly, then the outfielder may be able to play back a step or two.

Catching the Ball

The best place to catch a routine fly ball is just above eye-level (Fig. 8-2). If possible the ball should be caught with both hands. The fielder should try to catch the ball facing it, in a stride position. The

Fig. 8-2. *Whenever possible, fly balls should be caught with both hands, thumbs together and fingers pointing up. They should be caught above eye-level, and on the throwing arm side.*

glove should be in front of his face and on his throwing side. This places him in proper throwing position should he have to deliver the ball to a cutoff man after the catch. Basket catches, one-handed snatches, and fancy catches are not good. The simpler, the better.

On any ball below the belt, the fingers point down and the little fingers are together. When catching routine fly balls, the fingers point to the sky and the thumbs are together.

When running after a fly ball, an outfielder should follow three rules. First, he should run using his arms and not hold his glove out until the catch is to be made. An outfielder cannot run as far with his glove extended as he can if he pumps his arms at his sides. Secondly, he should run on the balls of his feet. If the ball appears to be moving up and down as he chases it, he is running on his heels. He must run smoothly. Third, he should try to run to the place where the ball will come down and not drift after it at three-quarter speed. An outfielder can never be sure when the wind will carry the ball a bit farther than he expected. A good drill for upper-division players to help stop them from drifting after the ball, and one that is a lot of fun, is to have them attempt to catch fly balls behind their backs. To do this they will hurry into position for the catch. Of course the purpose of this drill is to have the player run, not drift, into position to catch the ball. The actual reception of the ball behind the back takes practice, but the real point of the drill is to see how intent a youngster can get while waiting to catch a fly ball.

Another dangerous procedure is to backpedal after a fly ball. Footwork can become troublesome when backing up. The procedure shown in Figure 8-3 is definitely incorrect. With the ball hit directly over his head, the outfielder should take the first step back with the foot on his glove side (left foot for the right-hander and right foot for the left-hander). This step is followed by the other foot well in front of the leading foot. This is the most difficult play for outfielders and requires quite a lot of practice.

On balls hit to the side of the outfielder but over his head as well, he pivots on both feet in the direction he wants to go. His first step is with the foot nearest the ball (Fig. 8-4). Remember, in going deep for a fly ball, an outfielder will find his job easier if he runs to the spot where he thinks the ball will come down and waits for it there. He should be expected to glance over his shoulder to check on the flight of the ball. If he should happen to turn the wrong way, or if the flight of the ball changes, he should not turn so that he is momentarily backpedaling to correct himself.

He should instead turn as a football defensive back would, never taking his eyes off the ball. A coach can easily work on the proper mechanics of going back on the fly ball by tossing the ball well over each outfielder's head. This drill, often called the football toss, is

Fig. 8-3. *This player is backpedaling after a ball hit over his head. This procedure usually means trouble. He should turn and run to where he thinks the ball will come down.*

Fig. 8-4. *Catching balls hit deep is a difficult play. The outfielder must pivot on both feet in the direction he wishes to go and take his first step with the foot nearest the ball.*

excellent for lower-division players who are just learning to catch fly balls (Fig. 8-5).

Communication

Every coach has had the aggravating experience of watching an easy fly ball fall in between two outfielders when either one could have caught the ball.

Outfielders must help each other by calling loud and clear for all fly balls. As soon as he is absolutely sure he can catch the ball, the fielder must call for the ball, "I've got it; I've got it!" He should continue to call for the ball until he hears the other fielders call his name. Even when outfielders are sure of who is going to catch the ball, they must help one another. Outfielders should shout to each other how far they are from a fence or an out-of-play area. They should also yell where the throw will go before the ball is caught (Fig. 8-6).

Fig. 8-5. *The football-toss drill is excellent for teaching outfielders the proper footwork in going after balls laterally and behind them. This drill is also good for lower-division players who are just learning to catch fly balls.*

Fig. 8-6. *Outfielders must tell one another where to throw the ball. They can also offer verbal help in the form of a warning if a fence or barrier is near.*

Fly balls in which an outfielder is coming in and an infielder is going back can be troublesome. Confusion can be held to a minimum if the following rules are observed. First, the outfielder coming in has the right of way and should try for the ball until he is sure he cannot get it. He then tries to avoid the infielder by rolling off to a side and hitting the dirt. If the infielder hears the outfielder call for the ball, he moves off to the side and allows the outfielder room to catch the ball. Secondly, and very important, no one should call for the ball until it is in its downward flight. Sometimes an overaggressive ballplayer calls for the ball too soon and his teammates give up. Then the wind changes the direction of the ball and it falls to the ground.

Fielding Ground Balls and Throwing

There are two methods by which an outfielder should field ground balls. The first is when there are no runners on base or when a quick throw is not necessary. He should drop to one knee and leave no room for the ground ball to get through. Since no throw has to be made other than a soft relay to an infielder, the outfielder can follow the ball into his glove with both eyes on the ball. He should anticipate a bad hop and not be surprised by a sudden change in the path of the ball. Since many youth-league fields are maintained poorly, getting down and carefully blocking a ground ball is a must.

If a runner is advancing while the ground ball is moving toward an outfielder, then he must field the ball like an infielder. The ball must be fielded in front of him. The glove should be in contact with the ground until the ball takes its last hop. This way there should be no reason for a ball getting under the glove. The outfielder should run very hard until he gets to within five or six feet of the ball. He then must slow down, get his body under control and attempt to field the ball with both hands. If the field is rough, it will be necessary to sacrifice body momentum for a sure-fielded ball. Too many outfielders rush so much that they fumble the ground ball and no play can be made.

Every outfielder should feel that the ball will get past the infielders and he should be charging hard until he slows down to get his body under control.

Once a ground ball has been picked up or a runner has tagged up after a fly ball, proper throwing technique is necessary.

One of the most thrilling plays in all of sports occurs when an outfielder attempts to catch a runner at home plate. Coaches and players alike soon learn to respect the arms of many players and to take advantage of the poor throwing of many other players.

Coaches should stress accuracy rather than throwing strength. A hard throw that goes over the cutoff man's head and doesn't get the runner only allows another runner to advance. A very strong throw that bounces in front of an infielder's feet is tough to pick up. The best throws are those that bounce once before reaching an infielder. There are occasions when a player can throw all the way, but if the throw has too much of an arc, chances are it will arrive too late.

The ball should be gripped across the seams so it will rotate and stay on a true trajectory. It must be thrown from over the top so that it leaves the hand with top spin. If the ball is thrown sidearm, the rotation of the ball will be similar to that of a slice in golf, which occurs when the open face of a club head hits the golf ball. Proper throwing form is shown. Note that the throwing arm is away from the body so that the outfielder can bring the ball back and throw it in one continuous motion. The elbow comes back first, and the forearm trails back from the elbow. As the elbow leads the way, the arm, wrist and hand are brought forward. The throwing arm is whipped through in a free-and-easy follow-through, coming straight forward and then down across the body.

In addition to overthrowing the cutoff man, many youngsters throw to the wrong base. This is less likely to happen if the outfielder will ask himself, "Where am I going to throw the ball if I get it?" before each pitch. His teammates must help him also by shouting out which base to throw to.

General Information

The majority of major-league outfielders prefer a long-fingered glove with considerable webbing and a deep pocket. While infielders want to catch and throw the ball quickly, outfielders are not required to do this very often.

Should there be a fence in the outfield, the outfielder must run to the fence and then locate the ball. This would be better than trying to look for the ball and feel for the fence at the same time. Coaches should fungo balls or throw them off the fence so outfielders can practice reacting to a possible game situation.

With the winning run on third base and fewer than two outs in the last half of the last inning or any extra inning, a foul fly should not be caught unless the outfielder is positive he can throw out the runner. However, if the defensive team is ahead or it is early in the game, the ball can be caught with a runner on third. The score, the inning, and the way the game seems to be going should enter into the decision.

Each outfielder should consider any ball hit to an adjacent outfielder as a ball he will have to back up. Each outfielder must move somewhere on every play. The left fielder should back up every throw to second base. The right fielder should back up almost every throw to first base. He should also back up throws to second base from the third baseman and shortstop.

Playing a fly ball that is hit into the line of the sun can be a problem. If the ball is going directly in the line of the sun it is best to

Fig. 8-7. An alert right fielder and first baseman can team up to get a runner at first on a hard single to right field.

shade the eyes with the free hand so that the outfielder will have his glove hand free for the catch. If the ball only passes through the sun's glare then the outfielder can shade his eyes with his glove and look through the webbing of the glove. The important coaching point is that youngsters should not follow the ball directly through the line of the sun or they will be blinded temporarily and unable to make the catch.

On a base hit to right field, the right fielder may be able to throw the runner out at first base (Fig. 8-7). If the first baseman and the right fielder are alert, they can team up and get a slow runner on a hard single to right field.

Generally, an outfielder does not attempt a diving one-handed catch unless he must prevent the winning run from crossing the plate on a base hit late in the game. To make a diving catch, stay relaxed, double up, and roll as you hit the ground. A coaching point is to make sure the elbow of the glove hand is fully extended to prevent the ball from being jarred loose when hitting the ground.

I'm sure that by now you know that the outfield is a spot for a player with mental toughness, someone who can concentrate and stay in the ball game every pitch.

IX. Hitting and Bunting

Most youngsters will find batting as much fun as any part of baseball. Baseball fans at all levels enjoy games that include a lot of hits—games in which quite a few runs are scored. Nothing in sports can arouse more excitement than the winning run coming around third base.

The most popular major league baseball players have always been the greatest hitters. Everyone loves to hit, and baseball at all levels needs more good hitters. Then why don't we have more youngsters who can hit? There are two reasons.

First, hitting a baseball is the most difficult single skill in sports. Let me give you an example of just how difficult. Rod Carew, formerly of the California Angels, was the most recent major-leaguer to reach the 3,000-hit club. Everyone recognizes this as a great sports feat. Carew went to bat over 10,000 times. He was successful just about 30 percent of the time. This means he made an out, or was unsuccessful approximately seven out of ten times he came to bat. Yet he was only the fifteenth player in the history of baseball to reach this plateau. If a football quarterback completed only 30 percent of his passes, he would not last long. If a receiver dropped 70 percent of the passes thrown to him, he too would be replaced. Basketball players must be more successful than 30 percent with their shooting. A tennis player who only returned 30 percent of the balls served to him would surely be easy to defeat.

Hitting a baseball requires great physical skill. Strength and quickness with one's hands are necessary. Keen eyesight and excellent hand-eye coordination are most important. Ted Williams, one of the greatest hitters of all time, had better than twenty-twenty visual acuity. He was also a jet fighter pilot in the Korean War. He was six feet three inches tall and exceptionally strong.

The second reason why there are very few good youth-league hitters is that youngsters do not take enough batting practice. Not only was Williams gifted physically, but he studied the science of hitting and tried to get as much information as he could from every source. He took more batting practice than any man who ever played the game. A hitter has only two-fifths of a second to make up his mind whether or not to swing at the ball. To make adjustments as the ball is in flight, and to have a consistently good swing, the batter must have an awful lot of practice. Most young players just go to bat two or three times each game and rarely take batting practice.

Whether great hitters are born or made may never be settled. There is no doubt, however, that youngsters can become better hitters by taking more batting practice and receiving better hitting instruction.

Bat, Grip and Stance

There is no definite size bat for any particular individual. Each player must select a bat that is comfortable for him. Weight is probably the most important factor. Each player must select a bat on the basis of feel. A hitter picks up a bat and likes the feel of the handle. He sees that it is not too thick or too thin. The most important teaching point is to tell the youngster that a heavy, thick bat will not propel the ball any further than a lighter, thinner bat. Youngsters usually select a bat that is too heavy, feeling they can hit the ball further with it.

Most youth-league bats are anywhere from twenty-eight to thirty-three inches long. They weigh twenty-seven to thirty ounces. The majority of hitters are better off with a heavier bat choked up an inch or two than a lighter bat swung from the very end.

Bats made of aluminum and graphite are very common now. These bats last longer than conventional wood bats. While the sound of the ball hitting the bat may not be exactly the same as it would be using a wooden bat, the results are amazingly improved.

After having selected the bat, each hitter must then consider the grip. A large number of young players grip the bat incorrectly. While no two players have the same shape hands or the same length fingers, they all should attempt to hold the bat in such a way as to get the necessary wrist action. Most players should line up the middle knuckles of both hands (Fig. 9-1A). Adjusting by taking a few preliminary swings, a player may find that his knuckles are not perfectly in line. If this grip feels comfortable, then he should stay with it. At no time should he grip the bat so as to find the large set of knuckles lined up (Fig. 9-1B).

One of the most common faults of youngsters is gripping the bat too far back in the palms of the hands. The bat should be held with the fingers as much as possible. To arrive at the proper position of the bat in the hand, the player should place the bat across the middle knuckles on the face of his fingers and roll it toward the palm of his hand (Fig. 9-2). A right-handed hitter will use his left hand, a left-handed hitter his right hand. He then places the other hand in a similar position on the bat above the bottom hand. The bat should be located between the first two knuckles and should barely touch the palms of the hand. Don't let your players grip the bat too tightly.

Fig. 9-1 A&B. *In A, the bat is gripped correctly with the middle knuckles of both hands lined up. The wrists are cocked, the bat held in the fingers and slightly choked. In B, the large set of knuckles are lined up. This prevents proper wrist action.*

Fig. 9-2. *The proper grip is obtained by placing the bat across the middle knuckle of the bottom hand. Close the fingers as if shaking hands with the bat. The top hand is then placed in a similar position above the bottom hand.*

Remember, the feel of the bat should be in the fingers. Bats gripped too far back in the hands will prevent proper wrist action.

A hitter who chokes the bat (Fig. 9-1A) is more likely to find success than one who swings the bat from the very end. He may lose a little long-ball power, but choking will help gain bat control, which is more important. The hands are not usually spread apart. However, if the hitter finds success with the hands spread slightly, there is no need to change his grip.

Bats and grips look pretty much alike. Their differences are so slight it is hard for coaches and fans to see. But a batter's stance can be seen from anywhere in the ball park. The coach has an excellent opportunity to help each hitter find his proper stance.

Most young hitters should start out with their feet even. The most balanced stance is one in which the feet are shoulder-width apart. The weight should be equally distributed on the balls of the feet (Fig. 9-3). The bat should be still and the head stationary. The hitter must look over his front shoulder without tilting his head. The best hitters move their heads very little.

The coach should look for some common flaws. Young hitters have their weight too far back on their heels very often. Other times they cradle the bat (Fig. 9-4) so it is wrapped around the head. This

Fig. 9-3. Here is a normal batting stance. Check to see that the end of the bat is straight up, body erect, arms comfortably away from the body. The weight should be evenly distributed on the balls of the feet.

Fig. 9-4. A common batting flaw is that of cradling the bat. The end of the bat is not pointing straight up. The batter will not be able to bring the barrel of the bat around in time to meet the pitch.

makes the swing too long and prevents the hitter from getting around on the ball.

The hitter should assume a slight bend in the knees. A hitter who has his hips and butt sticking out too far will tend to be too rigid. Usually he is on his heels as well. Each hitter must try to maintain a relaxed position.

Usually the hands gripping the bat are at shoulder height and away from the body in a comfortable position. Often a young hitter keeps his hands too high and the bat too far from his body (Fig. 9-5). This leaves him very tense. If his arms are at shoulder height, he will only have to swing at pitches that are below the bat, since all those above will be balls. From this position he will start his all-important stride and swing.

Fig. 9-5. Batters who try to get their arms too far away from their bodies are too rigid. The bat is held too high by this batter. His hands should be even with his shoulders.

Stride and Swing

As the pitch moves toward the batter, he takes a short step with his front foot just before he begins his swing. The stride should be about six inches. It should be toward the pitcher, regardless of where the ball is pitched (Fig. 9-6).

A short stride enables the batter to keep his body under control. The purpose of the stride is to keep the body weight back. A batter who overstrides will have his body weight forward at the time the bat meets the ball. If his body weight is ahead of his swing, he has nothing left to hit the ball with but his arms. This batter is lunging at the ball. He usually hits off his front foot (Fig. 9-7). This hitting flaw is very difficult to correct. The hitter must discipline himself through many rounds of batting practice to "stay back" and wait on the pitch. You may find success by having him keep most of his weight on his back foot. He still must concentrate on not striding until the ball has been pitched. When he does stride, he must try to keep his bat back. A hitter with a long stride might be able to hit the ball if he does not commit his bat with his striding foot.

A stride box is one of the best teaching aids to prevent overstriding. Four two-by-four pieces of wood are needed. The two longer pieces run thirty-six inches lengthwise and are nailed to the two shorter pieces which are twenty-four inches wide. Extra two-by-fours are needed to insert into the box to accommodate the differences in

Fig. 9-6. *A good stride is about six inches. A batter begins his swing a slight fraction of a second after his stride.*

Fig. 9-7. *This batter has stridden too far. His body weight is too far forward. Lunging at the ball and hitting off the front foot is a difficult habit to break.*

individual stride lengths. To use the stride box the batter simply lays the structure on the ground and then steps in to do any number of drills which are mentioned throughout this chapter.

Sooner or later a youth-league coach runs into a youngster who "steps in the bucket." This batter, if right-handed, steps toward the third baseman as he strides, instead of at the pitcher. He may have been hit with a pitch before or he may lack confidence in his ability to be successful as a hitter. The first correction is for the coach to help the youngster rid himself of fear. Check to see that the hitter has a batting helmet that fits properly. Emphasize that the batting helmet will offer maximum protection. Then teach the youngster how to get out of the way of a pitch. If the hitter knows he is protected, and he has the ability to get out of the way of an inside pitch, then he is more likely to step at the pitcher.

To get out of the way of an inside pitch, a right-handed batter should turn his left shoulder toward the plate. He should continue to look at the ball as long as possible. When it is obvious that he must hit the ground, the batter takes the bat down with him, and hits the ground on his stomach (Fig. 9-8, A, B and C). Getting out of the way of a pitch in this manner prevents the batter from exposing any vital parts to the ball. If the batter attempts to block the ball with his hand, or if he goes down on his back, part of his body and his head are exposed. The hitter takes his bat down with him so that he will not land on it or have it land on him. This also prevents the ball from hitting the bat. Batters must practice getting out of the way of a pitch. Actually youngsters love the "bomber" drill. The coach lines up all the players in soft grass. When he yells "Down!" all the players pretend to get out of the way of a pitch. After the players have practiced this, the coach takes one batter at a time on the side. They come up as if they were at bat, helmet and all. Throwing tennis balls against a backstop, the coach pretends to be an opposing pitcher. He throws high and inside, and the youngsters practice getting out of the way (Fig. 9-9). The drill is especially important to the youngster who "steps in the bucket." He must gain confidence in his ability to get out of the way of a pitch.

If this doesn't work, another way to help the bucket hitter is to start him with an open stance. That is, with his foot already in the bucket (Fig. 9-10). While he cannot get out of the way in the manner explained above, he should have increased confidence because he is already facing the pitcher. However, he now has no place to stride except straight ahead, and if he can get a piece of the ball at all, he'll gain confidence, Remind him that this is only a temporary batting stance and that he can go back to his old one as soon as he learns to stride at the pitcher.

Don't put bats, books, bricks or anything else behind the batter's front foot in an effort to get him to step toward the pitcher. The batter

Fig. 9-8 AB&C. The hitter starts to get out of the way by turning his body to the inside. Note that no vital parts of the body are exposed. Each coach must have his players practice this.

Fig. 9-9. *The "Bomber" drill is a lot of fun. The drill is especially necessary for youngsters who need confidence in their ability to get out of the way of a pitched ball.*

Fig. 9-10. *A temporary measure to help the hitter who "steps in the bucket" is to have him face the pitcher with an open stance. This usually works best for lower-division players.*

will stride through the barrier anyway, and he might get hurt in the process.

Another common batting flaw is for the youngster to pull his head out as he swings. He fails to watch the ball hit the bat, because he is usually looking to left field (Fig. 9-11). The youngster is usually swinging too hard. The habit is easy to break if the coach will make this youngster practice hitting the ball to the second baseman. The batter must follow the ball and keep his head in if he is going to hit the ball to right field. The batter must also be reminded not to swing so hard. A really fine drill to insure that the batter will keep his head in when he swings is to have him take batting practice with his glove on his head. If the glove drops off, he is probably pulling his head out and swinging too hard (Fig. 9-12).

One of the most common hitting flaws at any level is uppercutting. A swing should be level, or in many cases slightly down. Only the strongest players can swing up and consistently be good hitters. These players propel the ball out of the park.

When a batter uppercuts at the ball, his left elbow comes out and the knob of the bat goes up. The back shoulder and the barrel of the bat both dip (Fig. 9-13). Only the bottom of the ball can be hit. A pop fly will be the result.

Fig. 9-11. *The player who pulls his head out cannot keep his eyes on the ball. He is usually overswinging.*

Fig. 9-12. *A drill to combat head pulling is to have the batter take batting practice with his glove on his head.*

Fig. 9-13. *The most common flaw of hitters at any level is uppercutting. Batters who hit the ball up have less chance of reaching base safely than batters who hit line drives and ground balls.*

Youth-league players should be discouraged from hitting fly balls. Line drives and ground balls are more likely to help the team. A ground ball not only has to be fielded cleanly, but it must also be thrown well to get an out. A fly ball need only be caught—no throw is necessary. There is less chance for the defense to make an error on a fly ball.

Any ball in the strike zone can be hit with a level or downward swing. To show a youngster that he can swing level, have him use the "hit-down" drill (Fig. 9-14). This is probably the best all-around hitting drill except for batting practice. A player lobs the ball just in front of the plate to a teammate who concentrates on hitting the middle or top half of the ball. If the ball is a line drive or a ground ball, then he has succeeded. If the ball is hit up into the air, he has hit its underside. This drill can be expanded to include low and outside pitches, high and inside pitches, change-ups, and all other pitches as well. The player tossing the ball need only throw it at different parts of the strike zone to have the batter practice swinging at all types of pitches. The ball is lobbed underhand from a distance of six to eight feet. The batter can hit the ball into a screen or out into the field where his teammates can field it.

Still another hitting flaw is hitching, or dropping the bat and hands as the ball is pitched. The batter doing this feels he can get more force into the swing. But the movement of the bat and hands makes it more difficult to hit the ball. Many hitters have been successful in spite of a hitch in their batting style. If a youngster can hit the ball consistently with a slight hitch, then allow him to continue.

Fig. 9-14. *The best hitting drill except for batting practice is the "hit-down" drill. A coach can watch a batter's swing as he hits all kind of pitches tossed by a teammate.*

When the arms are extended properly, the top hand should roll over after impact. The ball should be met just in front of the plate. The batter must rotate his hips so his belly button is facing the pitcher (Fig. 9-15). His front leg should be stiff, and he should be pushing off his back foot. Good hip rotation is what gives the hitter bat speed. Bat speed enables the batter to hit the ball with authority.

The head of the bat must be whipped forward as if the batter were going to throw it at the pitcher. Many young players are really afraid to whip the bat. Remind them that it's not how hard they swing that counts, it's how fast they swing. To get the youngsters to know the feeling of whipping the bat, have them actually throw the bat while lined up in the outfield. When using this drill, place a target like a batting tee about fifteen yards away. From his normal batting stance, the player whips the bat at the target. He concentrates as if he were swinging at a pitch right down the heart of the plate. If the bat goes up too high, then he is probably lowering his back shoulder.

Be careful when the batters get set to throw. Make sure everyone is out of the way. Youngsters just beginning this drill have a tendency to hold on to the bat too long. Encourage them to actually hit the target, but they must whip the bat. Don't let them throw it softly. Their body weight should be back. If they are on their front foot when they throw the bat, they will very likely be lunging when they get up to the plate and try to hit a pitched ball.

Fig. 9-15. *The batter must open up his hips. His front leg should be partially rigid. His wrists will roll over after impact and the bat should end up in the middle of his back.*

Another common hitting flaw is sweeping the bat. The hitter has a "slow bat" as a result of too long a swing. The bat arc starts behind the hitter's back shoulder in a wide, long arc taking extra time to get to the contact spot. A drill to correct this fault is to have the player face the fence and measure a distance of one bat's length. From this position the hitter concentrates on a compact swing. If he is sweeping, the bat will hit the fence.

After the batter has opened his hips and gripped the bat, he rolls his wrists after contact and follows through. A good follow-through provides extra force on each batted ball. The arms swing around to the rear and the bat ends up in the middle of the back (Fig. 9-16). The hitter should have good balance and follow-through in the direction the ball was hit. Be alert for the player who sweeps at the ball. This batter usually has the bat too far back in the palms of his hands. When he swings at the ball, it is impossible for him to break his wrist after contact. When he follows through, the bat ends up against his left shoulder rather than in the middle of his back (Fig. 9-17). The sweep hitter uses only his arms when he hits the ball. He rarely hits

Fig. 9-16. *Here is a good follow-through. The bat is in the middle of the back.*

Fig. 9-17. *This batter is a sweep hitter. He doesn't turn his wrist over after contact. The bat is too far back in the palms of his hands.*

the ball to the opposite field. This youngster should be made to swing in front of the coach, who makes sure the top hand comes over and the bat ends up in the middle of the batter's back. He should use the hit-down drill often, with the coach checking his hands and his follow-through.

Use of the Batting Tee

The batting tee is the best teaching aid for young hitters. If your league does not have a batting tee you can make one very easily. A piece of pipe one and a half inches in diameter and three feet long should be cemented into a can. Now all that is needed is a rubber hose about two feet long and one inch in diameter. Put the hose on the pipe and you are ready to go.

Each player must first be able to hit a stationary ball correctly before he goes up to the plate to hit a pitched ball. The batting tee can be used to correct any of the hitting flaws already mentioned. It can also be used to practice hitting pitches in different parts of the strike zone. The rubber hose can be raised or lowered to simulate a high or low pitch. The batter can move closer to the tee or farther from it to simulate an inside or outside pitch.

Batters can hit a regulation baseball at the infielders, or they can hit the ball into a backstop where no fielders are needed. The ball should be hit dead center, and the tee itself should not be touched. Don't be alarmed if the batter hits the tee with his first few cuts. Make him practice every day with the tee. High-school and college ball players and many professionals use the batting tee as a valuable teaching aid. It is also an excellent device for the batter who is in a batting slump.

If space is limited and no backstops are available, an enterprising coach can use a plastic ball attached to the bottom of the tee with a string about twenty feet long. These balls are available in any toy store. The batter can take his normal cut as in Figure 9-18, A and B. The ball will travel only twenty feet, of course, but the players and coach can tell if the hitter took the proper stance, swing and follow-through. Safety precautions should be used, as lower-division players tend to get too close to the batter at the tee. While the plastic ball will not hurt them, the batter might accidentally let go of his bat.

After the players get adept at hitting the ball off the tee, the coach can use an eye patch to make sure they stay adept. To ensure that the batter is watching the ball, place an eye patch on his right eye if he is right-handed. Now he'll have to watch the ball very closely and keep his head in there if he wants to hit the ball properly.

Fig. 9-18 A&B. *In A, the batter starts his swing at a plastic ball. A 20-foot string is attached to the ball and tee. While the batter can take his normal swing, you can see in B that the ball will not travel very far.*

An excellent practice drill is to divide your players into three teams with four or five on each. Send one man up to bat using the tee. Place the other eight or ten players on defense. Let each team have three outs while hitting off the tee. Rotate the teams and play about three full innings.

General Information

When a player goes up to bat, he should be looking to hit a specific pitch. This is not guess-hitting; this is thinking along with the pitcher. Most youth-league pitchers throw a fastball on the first pitch. The batter should set for a fastball and let any other pitch go by. He should prepare to hit a fastball on the outside portion of the plate. If the ball is inside, he can adjust, but if he is looking for an inside pitch and the pitch is outside, he has already committed himself. So the batter should always set for the express (a fastball) and look for the ball to come over the outside portion of the plate. He should never swing at any pitch that fools him unless he has two strikes. With two strikes, he should choke the bat even more and just look to make contact. Remember, a strike-out doesn't allow the defense to make an error. In order to force the defense into making mistakes, your team must move the ball.

Many youngsters are confused as to which pitches are actually strikes and which pitches are balls. I know it appears that many umpires seem confused about this also, but we'll let that go for now. A strike is any pitch that passes over home plate between the batter's armpits and the top of his knees when he assumes his natural stance. Every hitter must know the strike zone. If a batter starts swinging at pitches a few inches out of the strike zone, he increases his strike zone by quite a margin and makes the job of the pitcher a lot easier. Since most youngsters do not know the strike zone, they should always use the "strike zone" drill. Take four players and have them rotate between pitching, catching, batting and umpiring (Fig. 9-19). The pitcher throws from about forty feet away. Of course the batter never swings at any of the pitches. As the pitch crosses the plate, all four players call the pitch as an umpire would. Soon many players realize that pitches they thought were balls are actually strikes. The players should change positions after about twenty pitches. Positioning themselves as catchers, pitchers, and umpires, in addition to batters, gives them a realistic look at each pitch.

Pete Rose of the Cincinnati Reds was an exceptionally successful switch-hitter. Rose learned to switch-hit as a ten-year-old Little League ballplayer. Ballplayers best suited to become switch-hitters are usually right-handed hitters with good speed who are having trouble hitting one way. It is not usually a good idea to make a left-handed batter a switch-hitter. The advantage of switch-hitting is that the batter will never face a pitcher who throws from the same side he bats from. A left-handed batter will see mostly right-handed pitching anyway. He should concentrate on more practice against left-handed pitching rather than trying to switch-hit. The earlier one learns to switch-hit, the better. However, if the youngster is having trouble

Fig. 9-19. The "strike zone" drill is used to help all players learn which pitches are strikes. All the players call the pitch as an umpire would. They should rotate positions.

learning to switch-hit, do not force him to continue. Switch-hitting demands a great amount of coordination and ambidexterity. In addition, switch-hitting requires almost twice as much batting practice.

Strength is important in hitting a baseball. If two hitters have equal ability, the stronger one has the advantage. Lifting heavy weights is not necessary and without supervision might even be harmful. Simple strength-building devices like hand grips and small dumbbells are excellent if used regularly. An excellent strength-building device for hitting and throwing is the wrist roller (Fig. 9-20). A coach or player can make this device by cutting a broomstick handle to one foot in length and drilling a hole in the center. Three feet of rope is needed to attach a weight of two-and-a-half or five pounds. With his arms fully extended, the player raises the weight by twisting the broomstick handle in his hands. When he gets the weight up to the stick, he lets it down in the same fashion.

Isometric exercises are very good for building strength. An exercise that can be used at the park or at home is to have the batter push his bat against an immovable object for six seconds. At the park, a dugout post makes a good immovable object (Fig. 9-21). At

Fig. 9-20. *The wrist-roller device is excellent for increasing strength for both hitting and throwing. The device is easy to make.*

Fig. 9-21. *Isometric exercises are good for increasing strength. Here the batter pushes his bat against an immovable object for six seconds.*

home a doorway can be used. A player should also swing a heavy bat at home. He need not swing at a ball. Instead, making sure there is plenty of room, he swings at imaginary pitches in all parts of the strike zone. This will increase strength and improve his swing.

Each field should have a safe place for the next hitter to loosen up before he bats. This is called the on-deck circle. The on-deck circle should be complete with a lead bat or a weight to place on the end of the batter's regular bat. Also in the on-deck circle should be a rosin bag or pine-tar to aid in gripping the bat, and a towel. The batter should be able to swing his bat and loosen up his shoulders. He should also watch the pitcher and see if the pitcher is giving away any of his pitches. The on-deck hitter has the responsibility of helping a teammate who is scoring by telling him whether or not to slide. Since no base coaches can help a runner on a play at home plate, the on-deck hitter should motion for him to slide from a position behind home plate directly in front of the runner. If it is not necessary for the runner to slide, the on-deck hitter holds his hands up.

The hit-and-run play is a very good teaching tool for young hitters. With a runner on first base and the coach signaling for the hit-and-run, the batter knows he must swing at the very next pitch. He should not try to hit the ball any place in particular, but knowing he must make contact to protect the base runner will help him mentally. The runner going to second as he would on a steal is more likely to make it safely if the batter hits a ground ball. This play is used only when the runner cannot steal second on his own, or when the hitter might need the extra help of knowing he must swing at a specific pitch.

A good selling job on the part of the coach can help alleviate many batting problems. The coach must speak with confidence. He must be able to convince the youngsters that the home-run swing is not necessary—that contact is more important than power. The coach must make the youngster want to practice his batting. Each youngster must be convinced that hitting is a difficult skill and must practice as much as possible.

Bunting

The major-league emphasis on the long ball and the big inning has caused the art of bunting to be neglected. However, every year, as the playoff games begin and the World Series starts, we see the professionals bunting in spite of the lively ball and artificial surfaces. The bunt will not score as many runs as the home run, but it is very often instrumental in the outcome of an important game. At the youth-league level, when a bunt is laid down and fielded, a throw must be made to an infielder who is moving to cover a base. In addition, split-second decisions have to be made as to which base to throw to.

Bunting is an important weapon for every team's offense. Well-executed bunts can break a game wide open. When teaching youngsters to bunt, every coach must emphasize the word "sacrifice." The primary purpose of the sacrifice bunt is to advance a runner or runners. The batter who bunts the ball is not concerned with reaching base. He literally sacrifices himself to help the team's cause.

The first teaching point is to make sure the batter squares around properly. As the pitcher starts his motion to home plate, the batter takes a quick step forward with his left foot and follows with a long step with his right foot, so his feet are even as he faces the pitcher (Diag. 9-1). With his arms extended but not stiff he should hold the bat out in front of home plate, just below the shoulders. It should be at the upper part of the strike zone so he will not have to move it up to bunt a ball. All pitches above the bat will be balls and should be left alone. A pitch below the bat is better to bunt since the bat will be pushed downward and a pop-up is less likely (Fig. 9-22).

The upper hand should slide toward the fat part of the bat and come to rest just below the label. The fingers of the upper hand do not go around the bat. The thumb, index finger and middle finger make a groove in which the bat is held comfortably. The best method of helping youngsters learn to hold the bat properly is to use a bat that has tape exactly where you want the hands placed (Fig. 9-23). The part of the bat that is not supposed to be touched is painted black.

The height of the bat should be adjusted mostly by raising or lowering the knees. The actual bunt is performed in a manner similar

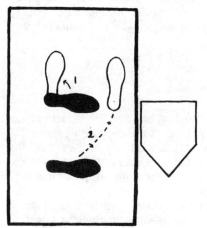

Diagram 9-1. *As the pitcher moves to the plate, the batter takes a quick step with his left foot and a longer step with his right foot so that his feet are even.*

Fig. 9-22. *When the ball is pitched, the batter should have his bat in front of the plate. More experienced bunters should try to get near the front of the batter's box. Note the foot pads, which are his normal batting stance. The bat should be held just below the shoulders.*

to catching a ball. The head of the bat should give a little as contact with the ball is made. A good technique to teach this to youngsters is to have them use the "glove-bat" (Fig. 9-24). Take an old glove and nail it to the end of a bat. Have the youngsters try to catch the ball with the bat. If they do not give a little, the ball will not stay in the glove. If batters won't give a little when contact is made on the actual bunt, the ball will be fouled off or bunted too hard.

Fig. 9-23. *A bat with tape wrapped in the exact location where the hands should be placed is a good teaching tool for beginning bunters.*

Fig. 9-24. Bunting a pitch is similar to catching a ball. The head of the bat must give a little as it meets the ball. The "glove bat" helps the beginning bunter remember this. An old glove is nailed to a bat, and the player tries to catch the ball with the bat.

The batter should attempt to bunt only at pitches that are strikes. The greatest danger in executing the sacrifice is bunting the ball up in the air. In addition to letting the high pitches go, the batter should concentrate on bunting the ball with the bottom half of the bat. If this is accomplished, the bunt must go into the dirt. A coach can help his players learn to do this by having them bunt with a "half-bat." This is a bat of which the top half has been cut away. Usually a cracked bat can be made into a good "half-bat" for bunting practice. If the player learns to bunt without the top part of the bat, he'll have no problem laying the ball down.

Generally speaking, with a runner on first the batter should attempt to bunt the ball close to the foul line on the first-base side. This is usually the best bunt because the first baseman has to wait until the ball is pitched before charging in. The third baseman can charge even before the batter squares around if he is sure of the bunt situation. However, most youngsters should bunt the ball where it is easiest for them to do so on any given pitch. However, with a runner on second, or runners on first and second, the batter should try at least once to bunt the ball past the pitcher so the third baseman will have to field it. This usually puts pressure on the defense, and many times the pitcher and third baseman get confused as to who should field the ball and all runners end up safe.

The suicide squeeze play is executed in the same manner as the sacrifice bunt. The only difference is that the batter **must** bunt the ball. The runner at third leaves as the pitcher's arm starts forward. The batter squares around and attempts to bunt the pitch anywhere on the ground. If the bunt is laid down, the runner usually will score.

However, if the bunt is missed, the runner will be tagged out. If the bunt is popped up, there is usually a double play. A safety squeeze is performed in much the same manner, except that the runner from third will not leave until the batter actually bunts the ball. In either squeeze play, the batter must be a good bunter. The runner at third must try not to give away the squeeze by leaving too soon. The batter, too, must not give away the squeeze or the pitcher might throw a very hard pitch to bunt.

The bunt-and-run can be an effective play. With a runner on first, the batter tries to lay down a bunt to the third baseman. The base runner, who broke on the pitch, rounds second base and continues to third, which will be unoccupied if the catcher or pitcher is not alert. A runner can score from second base if he breaks on the pitch and the ball is bunted well. If the ball is fielded by the third baseman, the runner can round third and continue toward home. It will require a good throw from the first baseman or the second baseman covering first to get the runner at the plate.

A fake bunt is always a good weapon. If you are undecided as to how your opponents will defend a bunt, then have your player square around as if he was going to bunt, and the defense will react. The batter can then see who is charging and who is staying back. On the next pitch he'll have a better idea of where to bunt the ball.

A hitter might surprise the defense and bunt for the base hit with no runners on base, or with two outs and a runner on third. Since sacrifice bunting starts the infielders in motion, a hitter should not drag bunt or push bunt until the very last instant. Bunting for a hit is often used when the third baseman is playing deep. The ball should be bunted close to the foul line and met by the hitter while he is on the move. Whether the batter is right-handed or left-handed, he should take a short step forward with his front foot as the ball is delivered so he can meet the ball in front of the plate. He should drop the bat down on the ball so the bunt will go into the dirt. The batter must watch the ball hit the bat. One mistake made by many hitters is that they try to bunt just any pitch for the base hit. Slower pitches, pitches on the outside portion of the plate, and low pitches are easiest to bunt. Do not have your players bunt just any pitch. Even if a signal for a bunt was given, don't make it a command to bunt that particular pitch; have the players consider the signal permission to bunt only if the pitch is good.

Youngsters love to have contests in which they can show their various abilities. A bunting game that your players will love is one in which they try to bunt the ball into a specific area and accumulate points. Divide your team in half, or let two captains select teams. Place six to nine bats down the third-base line as shown in Figure 9-25. If the ball is bunted inside the area marked off by the bats, give

Fig. 9-25. *Divide your team in half. Have them try to bunt the ball into the area marked off by the bats. Each team supplies its own pitchers or the coach pitches for both teams.*

the team five points. If it rolls over the last three bats, give the team three points. If the ball is bunted fair, give the team one point. Each team member should get at least three bunt attempts. If the coach can't pitch for both teams, then have each team supply its own pitcher. The team with the highest point total wins. The next day move the target area to the first-base line.

If a coach feels any play involving a bunt is called for, he should go ahead with it. Don't pay any attention to the second-guessers who always seem to know what should have happened after the play is over. If enough practice time is devoted to the fundamentals of bunting, the bunt will be an effective part of your team's offense. By using the bunt, your team can create many difficult situations for the defensive team, and if your opponents are not properly prepared, many mental mistakes and fielding errors will result.

X. Baserunning and Base Coaching

Baserunning is the most neglected part of almost every player's game. Many youngsters go an entire season without ever practicing sliding, taking a turn at a base, or baserunning situations.

A good base runner's value to his team is obvious. He can steal second instead of being bunted there. He can take an extra base on a hit. He can upset the defense because of his reputation as a runner so that missed ground balls and overthrows will seem to be showered upon him.

Qualifications of a Good Base Runner

Speed is a God-given talent. It can be improved, but not much. However, just being fast afoot will not make one a good base runner. Fast runners who do not have much experience have a way of sliding into a base that may already be occupied by a teammate. Intelligence and sound judgment are more important. Knowing the situation—like the number of outs, the strengths and weaknesses of the opposition, the inning and the score—contributes more to intelligent base running.

Proper running form includes running on the balls of the feet. The base runner should never run with his head down. His toes should point straight ahead. The arms should be pumping back and forth, not crossing over in front of the body. His hands should be open and his elbows bent at approximately right angles.

Aggressiveness and good instincts are very important. While instincts are more a natural trait than a learned one, they can be developed, to a degree, with practice and game experience. Aggressiveness can be aided by the coach who shows confidence in his player's ability to run the bases. Of course he must not find fault with base runners who take chances but are occasionally unsuccessful.

The ability to slide is another requisite for good baserunning. Youngsters can be taught to slide easier than adults. Sliding, once properly learned, is rarely forgotten. A player may get rusty, but a few short practice sessions can have him ready once again.

Running from Home Plate

A poor start from home plate can make the difference between being safe or out on a close play at first base. Every player must give 100 percent when running to first base. You can never tell when an easy ground ball will be booted. Naturally, each player must be reminded not to look at the ball. The runner should keep his eyes on first base.

After he has hit the ball, a right-hander should drop the bat behind him with his left hand, dip his chest slightly toward first, and take a short step with his right foot. He should keep the first few steps short, increasing the length gradually. A left-handed batter is closer to first base and has an advantage over a right-hander. Most left-handed hitters should use a crossover step with the left foot, pivoting on the right foot as they take off for first base.

The base runner should reach for the front edge of first base. He should not jump at the base (Fig. 10-1).

The only time sliding into first base is advisable is when the runner is trying to avoid a tag by the first baseman who was pulled off the base.

After he crosses the base, he should continue in a straight line for a few steps. Assuming he is safe, he should turn to his left so he is facing the field and can find the ball. Only if he attempts to go to

Fig. 10-1. *No! Don't jump at the base. Reach for the front edge of the base. After touching the base, continue for a few steps and then turn to the left to return to first base.*

second can he be tagged out. A base runner may overrun first in fair territory without jeopardy of being tagged out so long as he does not commit toward second base.

Another method of running to first base is used on a single or an apparent extra-base hit. The runner begins circling toward first about fifteen feet from the base. He does this by swerving to his right. He should approach the base at full speed. To avoid taking too wide a turn, he must lean in toward the pitcher's mound (Fig. 10-2). It doesn't matter which foot he touches the base with as long as he touches the inside portion of it. As he hits the base from the inside, he should turn as sharply as possible and head for second until he either sees that he cannot make it or is stopped by the base coach. Remember, do not have your runners break stride to hit the base with either the left or right foot. It is much better to emphasize hitting the inside portion of the base so they do not stray too far to right field on the way to second base.

Leading Off the Various Bases

Let me recognize the fact that many youth leagues have rules prohibiting leaving the base until the ball reaches the batter. While base runners in these leagues will start considerably differently from those in other leagues, there are still basic fundamentals for them to follow.

Fig. 10-2. *On a base hit, the batter leans in toward the pitcher's mound as he rounds the base. It doesn't matter which foot he touches with. Note the coach telling him to go to second base. The first baseman is watching to make sure the runner touches the base.*

In Little League and other leagues where the prohibition exists, the youngster should be touching the edge of the base with the ball of his right foot. He should be facing the next base in a stance with his hands hanging loosely at his sides. Do not allow him to rest his hands on his knees. His left foot should be a short stride in the direction of the next base (Fig. 10-3). As the ball reaches the batter, he should take one fast step with his right foot, another with his left, then one more with the right. His last step brings him to a position so he is facing the infield. If the catcher misses the ball or if the steal is on, he will continue to the next base. However, if he wants to return to the base because of a line drive or pick-off attempt, he can use the third step as a push-off to enable him to get back.

When a runner is on first base, he should never step off the base until he knows exactly where the ball is. He should also know the number of outs, the score, and whether there are other runners on base. As he relaxes with his foot on the base, he should check to see where the fielders are playing. He should also look to the coach in case a signal is to be given.

How far the runner will lead off will depend upon his own ability and the pitcher's ability to throw to first base. Usually the runner will use shuffle steps. He moves his right foot toward second base and then brings his left foot up behind, keeping both feet close to the ground. Normally the best lead is three steps. If this appears to be too short, the runner can add another half or whole shuffle step. When the lead is completed, the base runner is wise to put most of his weight on his left foot. This is a one-way lead, in which the runner

Fig. 10-3. *Here the runner demonstrates proper form in a youth league where rules prohibit the runner from leaving until the ball reaches the batter. Don't allow your runners to put their hands on their knees.*

tests the pitcher's move to first. If this lead proves satisfactory, or if a steal is in order, the runner uses a two-way lead, with the weight evenly distributed on the balls of his feet so he can go either way (Fig. 10-4).

A runner who is taking a maximum two-way lead must dive back to first when the pitcher throws over. He pivots on his left foot, pushing off and reaching for the outfield side of the base. The back is slightly arched as he stretches for the base with his right hand. As he reaches the base, his head is turned slightly toward right field so his helmet will offer protection in case of an errant throw.

If the runner can get back standing up, he should reach the base with his right foot. To do so he crosses over with his right foot, steps quickly with his left, and then touches the base with his right. This way his back will be toward the pitcher so he can see exactly where an errant throw goes. He is also protected, as no vital parts of his body are exposed to a possible missed throw by the first baseman.

Another type of lead is called the walking lead. The runner starts moving off the base a little later than in the previous method but keeps walking toward the next base using short steps. If the pitcher does not make him stop, he can get an excellent break for a steal.

The hidden-ball trick has been worked successfully many times. Even in professional ball, runners have been tagged out when they stepped off a base thinking the pitcher had the ball. One runner was tagged out when he was asked by the first baseman to step off and let him kick dirt off the base. The antidote for the hidden-ball trick is simple. Since the pitcher cannot assume a pitching position without

Fig. 10-4. *The runner should get his lead without having to cross his legs. He's in a slight crouch, his arms hanging loosely in front of him. His weight should be evenly distributed on the balls of his feet so he can go either way [two-way lead].*

the ball, the runner should stay on the base until the pitcher is about to start his stretch or windup. Of course, the base coach should help the base runner locate the ball immediately after he reaches first base.

When a left-handed pitcher is holding a runner on first base, the runner must make certain concessions. Normally, he should take a shorter lead. Because of the left-hander's step, umpires seldom call balks, so the runner must wait a little longer before shuffling off or breaking to steal. Of course, if the lefty doesn't have a move to first, it could be easier to get a good jump on him than on a right-hander.

Baserunning is the most undercoached and least understood phase of the game. This applies to baseball at all levels. For example, not many coaches will tell a runner what to do after he leads off a base and the ball is **not** hit. Many youngsters will stay in the same place as the pitcher throws the ball to home plate. The runner should take two shuffle steps, which will bring his weight down on his right foot as the ball passes the batter. He can then stop and get back to the base, or if the ball is hit he can continue.

Another good baserunning procedure is to have the runners occasionally use a false break. This is a two-step fake toward second base as the pitcher throws the ball to home plate. The runner does this quickly and aggressively, the defense will yell he is stealing, the catcher will get set to throw, and either the shortstop or second baseman will take a few steps toward second base. Sometimes the pitcher might even hurry his pitch because he thinks the runner is stealing. This chain reaction can be an asset to the offensive team. The runner should cross over with his left foot and step once with his right to complete the false break. He should start as soon as the pitcher makes his move to home plate.

A good way to lead off second base is the "first-base lead." The runner keeps his eyes on the pitcher's rear leg. He takes the same lead as if he were at first base with the first baseman at the bag. The advantage of this method is that the runner will never have to move back toward second unless the pitcher moves his rear leg. The base coaches need not warn him if the shortstop or second baseman cover the base, because his lead is short enough that he can get back even if they are positioned at the base before the pitch. When the ball is pitched, the runner takes two large shuffle steps toward third base.

Good base runners can take larger leads off second base,but the base coaches must warn them if the shortstop breaks for the base. Sometimes the runner can see the second baseman break for the bag. However, if the runner starts back for the base, the pitcher delivers the ball and the batter hits the pitch, the runner will not have a very good break for third.

When leading off third base, the runner should be in foul territory. He should start out a step or so farther away from the base than the third baseman. As the pitcher starts his windup, the runner should walk toward home plate. If the catcher catches the ball, the runner must stop on his right foot and return to the base, looking over his right shoulder at the ball. He should return inside the foul line to block a possible throw from the catcher. He must also learn to watch the throw back to the pitcher. If the throw is poor, he can break for home plate if no one is backing up the pitcher.

Some runners like to streak for home plate as the pitcher is in his windup. This rarely upsets the pitcher, and the runner usually goes back to third as the ball is pitched. As a result he is not moving in the proper direction to score on a passed ball or a ground ball.

If the ball is hit in the air with less than two outs, the runner should automatically get back. It is a sin to get doubled off third base on a line drive. If the ball turns out to be a base hit, the runner will score anyway.

There are two methods of tagging up at third base after a fly ball has been caught. Most upper-division players can turn toward the outfield and see for themselves when to leave. The ball of the left foot should be used to push off the base as the outfielder catches the ball. In the lower division and with upper-division players who do not have enough experience, the coach can help. He can align himself so he can see the outfielder and the runner can see him. He holds his right arm up, forming an "L." As the outfielder catches the ball, the coach brings his arm down vigorously. The runner will not leave until the coach moves his arm (Fig. 10-5).

Fig. 10-5. *Lower-division players may need the help of the third base coach when tagging up. The coach decides when they should leave the base, vigorously lowering his arm when the ball is caught.*

Stealing the Various Bases

Ty Cobb once said, "The runner loose on the basepaths is the most spectacular sight in baseball." No one challenged Cobb's record of ninety-six stolen bases in a single major-league season until Maury Wills stole 104 in 1962. Lou Brock, of the St. Louis Cardinals, broke Wills's record in 1974, at the age of thirty-five. Rickey Henderson holds the current record of 130, which he set in 1982 while playing with the Oakland Athletics. These and many other daring base runners have helped change the image of professional baseball from total power to speed and baserunning skill.

Although the home run is still baseball's big attraction, daring and aggressive baserunning has found an important place in the game.

When to steal is a very important part of the game. Usually the following general rules can be followed:

1. When your team is four or five runs behind, it is not a good idea to steal. Play for the big inning.

2. When your team is four or five runs ahead late in the game, it is usually in bad taste to attempt a steal. This could be considered rubbing it in.

3. A runner is more likely to steal with two outs than with one or none.

4. It is better to steal second base with a left-handed hitter up. The catcher has a tougher time setting up to throw.

5. It is better to steal on a curve ball than on a fast ball. The curve is a slower pitch.

6. It is not a good idea to steal with a weak hitter up and two outs. He may have to lead off the next inning.

Naturally the individuals involved determine whether the steal is a good idea. Most outstanding base runners steal at every opportunity. If the catcher is a poor thrower, or the pitcher doesn't hold the runners on well, then the steal is obviously in order.

While many youngsters have outstanding footspeed, young players with outstanding throwing arms are rare. It would seem logical to take an extra base or attempt a steal in many instances that would be bad risks in professional baseball. As a coach, you must do what is successful for your team. There is no rule of thumb for youth-league baseball coaches regarding baserunning.

When stealing second base, a player must concern himself with his lead, break, and sliding ability. The break for second base and the ability to run at top speed after only a few steps are the most important items.

Some base stealers watch the pitcher's shoulders as their key. Others watch the pitcher as a whole. The easiest method is to watch his heels. If he is going to throw to first base he will lift his right heel, and the runner should go back. When throwing to home plate, the pitcher will lift his left heel only, and the runner can break for second base.

The crossover step should be used by every base runner attempting to steal second base. He pivots on the ball of his right foot, then takes a crossover step with his left foot. He should swing his left arm vigorously to gain momentum for a quick start.

A really fine drill to practice the lead and break is shown in Figure 10-6. Place two, three, or four base runners at first base. Use a first baseman and a pitcher. The runners get their maximum two-way lead. They key the pitcher's heels. If the pitcher goes to first, they practice getting back to the base. If the pitcher throws home, they practice their break for second base. The coach stands about halfway to second base on the outfield side of the baseline. He can see if the runners all break at the pitcher's first move to home plate. He can also see which runner passes him first. The youngsters love competition.

Catchers can also practice throwing to second base, pitchers can work on their moves to first base, and first basemen can practice catching and tagging. The coach can also use this drill to have his

Fig. 10-6. *Runners must practice getting good leads and breaks off first base. Here the runners are watching the pitcher's heels. All the runners will react to the pitcher. If he throws to first, they go back. If he throws home, they break for second.*

runners practice the false break and to have the inexperienced ones practice shuffling off the base after the ball is pitched.

Stealing third base is probably easier than stealing second. However, if the runner is caught, a potentially easy run is removed, and for this reason most coaches do not have their runners attempt to steal third very often. With a right-handed batter the throw to third is a little more difficult for the catcher.

A good play when your runner is stealing third base is to have the batter square around and fake a bunt. Sometimes the third baseman will charge, leaving no one at third to receive the catcher's throw. The runner can watch the ball when he steals third, as he cannot in stealing second.

A steal of home is an exceptionally exciting play. It can be worked with a good base runner against a pitcher who is taking a full windup. It should never be used with fewer than two outs or with two strikes, since the batter has to swing if the pitch is a strike.

At the youth-league level, the steal of home can be attempted as the catcher throws back to the pitcher. If the runner takes a few steps off third and breaks for home as the catcher's arm starts forward, he has a good chance to make it. Many times catchers will make the mistake of not looking at the runner, or simply throwing the ball too slowly. The catcher should take a step or two toward the pitcher, look the runner back to third, and then return the ball to the pitcher with something on it. The pitcher should take a step or two toward the catcher as he waits for the return.

Sliding

Sliding is nothing more than controlled falling. Young players soon learn that it is a matter of dropping to the ground and letting their momentum do the rest. There are three purposes in sliding. One is to evade the tag, another is to stop at the base, and the third is to avoid a collision.

A base runner must learn when to slide. A general rule is that a runner going at top speed should begin his slide about six to eight feet from the base. As he goes into his slide, he must keep his hands up to avoid injuring his fingers. He should keep his chin close to his chest. Once a base runner decides to slide, he must continue to go through with it. **He must not change his mind.**

The only slide that a youngster needs to learn is the bent-leg slide. This slide is the safest, the easiest to learn, and gets you to the base the fastest (Fig. 10-7). This slide also allows a base runner to spring up quickly.

To start the youngsters learning the slide, the circle method of instruction shown in Figure 10-8 is recommended. The coach

Fig. 10-7. *The bent-leg slide is the easiest to learn and the safest, and gets the slider to the base the quickest way.*

Fig. 10-8. *The circle method of instruction is very good for beginning sliders. The coach can check the position of each player.*

positions himself in the center and checks to see that each player is in the proper position. Most players will naturally tuck their right legs underneath them. Usually left-handed boys will bend their left legs. It does not matter which leg is used. The bent leg is tucked underneath the extended one to make a figure four. The hands should be up, the fingers making a partial fist. The chin should be close to the chest. The boys should be reminded that their stomach muscles must hold them up as they slide. If they allow their upper backs to touch the dirt, they will not be able to slide well.

Sliding should be practiced in the soft outfield grass. Have the players who are wearing spikes remove them so they don't get caught in the grass. Do not strap down the bases. If a player slides too late, the base will move as his foot hits it. To help get the players to keep their hands up, the coach can use a bat as shown in Figure 10-9. As the players begin to slide, the coach lifts the bat up. To help the boys learn when to slide, the coach should be about six to eight feet from the base.

Another value of the bent-leg slide is that the runner may "pop up" after his front foot hits the base. He is then ready to go on to the next

Fig. 10-9. *Here the coach is using a bat to help his players learn to keep their hands up while sliding. They try to grab the bat as they slide underneath it, but the coach lifts it out of reach.*

base should the throw get away. To help players learn the pop-up slide, remind them that they must use their stomach muscles to keep their backs up. The force of hitting the base with the front foot will enable them to continue forward to a standing position. Two teammates can help a player up by standing on each side of him as he slides and giving him a lift as his front foot hits the base (Fig. 10-10).

Whether using the straight-in bent leg or the bent leg and pop-up, runners have to be reminded to take the weight of the fall on the bent leg. If they slide, rather than jump or leap, they will not get bruised. In sliding on the bent leg, they should keep low to the ground. The slider must keep his eyes on the base. If he allows his head to fall back, it will be difficult for him to slide.

Another type of slide, the head-first slide, is necessary when trying to get back to a base after a pick-off attempt. The slide can be used going into any base. It is especially good if the runner has an injury to his legs. However, this slide can be dangerous—not because the ball might hit the slider in the head, because all runners should wear batting helmets, but because a jumping defender might come down on his hands or arms with his spikes. Another reason is that players do not practice the head-first slide enough.

Fig. 10-10. *Teammates can help another player learn to "pop-up" by lifting him as his front foot hits the base.*

The runner must extend both arms toward the base and slide primarily on his chest and stomach (Fig. 10-11). His head must be up, and his back slightly arched. He must not leap at the base; he must stay low to the ground. This is a slide—not a dive! Diving causes injury to the chest and rarely allows the runner to effectively reach the bag. The head-first slide is only for youngsters who like to use it, and for those who can do it safely.

Baserunning Plays

The delayed steal is run when the coach or base runner feels the shortstop and second baseman are too far from second base. The base runner shuffles off after the pitcher throws to home plate. When the ball passes the batter, he breaks for second base. Although the catcher sees him go, there is no one at the bag to receive the throw. Players with average speed can run a delayed steal. Remember, the base runner must not break for second until the ball passes the batter.

Another form of the delayed steal can be used in the lower division. The runner waits until the catcher is about to throw the ball back to the pitcher; then he breaks for the next base. The coach must look for a catcher who is not paying attention to the runner.

When a team meets a catcher who has an excellent arm—one who loves to throw to the bases—they should try the halfway steal. The base runner takes two extra shuffle steps as the ball passes the batter, making the catcher think he can be picked off base. When the

Fig. 10-11. *The head-first slide is necessary when trying to get back to first base. It can also be used if the runner has an injury to his legs.*

catcher throws for the pick-off, the runner breaks for the next base. If the catcher drops the ball or simply does not throw, the runner should break for the next base anyway.

When a coach has runners on first and third, especially with two outs, he has an opportunity to run many plays. He can signal for a normal or delayed steal from first and have the runner on third react to the catcher's throw to second. This runner watches the throw come out of the catcher's hand; if the throw is very high, he breaks for home, but if it is low, he holds. The runner from first does not slide into second base but stops short of the bag and avoids being tagged as long as he can. The runner at third breaks for home if it appears the infielder with the ball has forgotten about him in his effort to get the youngster in the rundown. If he scores before the tag, the run counts.

Another play that is often successful with runners at first and third is the forced balk. The runner breaks for second as the pitcher starts to go into his stretch position. If the pitcher starts to throw to first, and stops, then it is a balk. If the pitcher steps off the rubber as he should, and throws to the shortstop, the runner from third breaks for home. Once again, the runner from first should get in a rundown.

Still another first-and-third play, one that is designed to take advantage of a poor-throwing first baseman, is the pickle play. The runner on first should take a larger lead than he normally would. He wants the pitcher to throw to first base. When the pitcher does throw over, the runner breaks for second base. The runner on third breaks for home if the first baseman throws to second. If the first baseman holds the ball, the runner from first base advances.

Whenever you have runners on first and third and fewer than two outs, the runner on first base should tag up and head for second on any fly ball. This is especially successful when the fly ball is caught in foul territory. The fielder usually forgets about the runner at third, and when the throw goes to second base, the runner from third can score. The runner headed for second should be sure he is not tagged out before the run scores. He must get into a rundown and avoid the tag as long as possible.

Youth-league coaches cannot pattern their strategies exclusively after that of the major leagues. Instead, each coach should employ a strategy based upon the maneuvers he feels his players are capable of performing. At the youth-league level, daring baserunning assumes a great strategic importance in a one-run game. Because of the weak and erratic throwing arms of younger players, daring baserunning can force the defense to throw the ball away. On any close play, the base runners will have an advantage.

Every player must have the desire to take an extra base. Daring baserunning should be instilled into each runner. Even in situations where it is impossible to advance, the runner should fake aggressively enough to draw a throw. The more the defense throws, the better the chance that they will throw the ball away.

Coaching the Bases

Coaching at first base and third base is important. In most leagues a manager or coach may occupy one of these positions. Most likely an adult would be better coaching third base. If you use a youngster, you must impress upon him the importance of good base coaching. Boys who love the game, especially if they are injured and cannot play, usually make excellent coaches.

Coaches should work with the base runner as soon as he drops the bat. On a batted ball to the infield, the first-base coach must encourage the runner to beat the throw. If the ball goes through the infield, the coach should tell the runner to take a turn instead of running past the base. If the ball is definitely a base hit, possibly even extra bases, the coach must move up in the coach's box and point toward second base while he yells instructions.

When the runner reaches first base safely, the first-base coach has several responsibilities. First, he must help the runner locate the ball. Second, he must let the runner know how many outs there are. Third, he must watch the head coach giving signals so that he will know what to say in case the runner asks for help.

The two main defensive players the first-base coach must watch are the pitcher and the first baseman. If the pitcher throws to first base, the coach must yell, "Back, back!" If the first baseman is playing behind the runner, instead of in front, then the coach must watch him.

In the time it takes the pitcher to get set between pitches, the first-base coach can remind the runner about the score and the importance of his run, keep him alert for a bunt or steal, and tell him to look to the coaches for signals. The first-base coach can be very helpful if the runner misses the signal from the third-base coach. He can simply tell him what he missed or repeat the signal himself. If no signal was given, the first-base coach can say, "Nothing on."

Third base is where all the coaching action is. It is difficult to be a good third-base coach without some study and practice. The best way to help a runner at second base is to watch both the shortstop and the second baseman. The runner should watch the rear leg of the pitcher. If the shortstop or second baseman breaks for the bag, the third-base coach yells, "Back, back!" If the coach thinks the infielder is just bluffing, then he doesn't say anything.

His most important job is helping the runner as he comes to third base. If it appears that the runner should go home, the coach moves toward home plate, moving his right arm in a complete circle. He should be yelling instructions also. He should be careful not to get too close to the baseline, or the runner might bump into him. His arm should move vigorously in a clockwise rotation. If there are other runners on base, the coach must run back to his position in the box to direct these runners.

If the runner has plenty of time to make it to third base, but can go no further, then the signal demonstrated in Figure 10-12 is used. Now the runner knows he can take a short turn because the ball is coming back into the infield.

If the throw is coming to third, and the coach does not want his runner to take a turn, he must point to the base with one hand and hold the other hand straight up. Now the runner knows that the throw is coming to third and he should not step off the base (Fig. 10-13).

On any close play, the coach will want his player to slide. Since the runner has his back to the action, he relies on the coach's decision. The decision must be firm and prompt. Figure 10-14 shows the proper form for the coach to use in signaling his player to slide into third base. It is not necessary to tell him which side to slide to. The straight-in bent-leg slide will be used. The coach must make his decision when the runner is a little more than halfway to third.

Fig. 10-12. *Here the runner has plenty of time to make it to third base. However, he cannot go any further because the ball is coming into the infield: The coach with his hands up is telling the runner to stand up and take a short turn at third base.*

Fig. 10-13. *The runner knows that the throw is coming to third. While he does not have to slide, he knows he should not leave the base once he touches it.*

Fig. 10-14. *The coach should be yelling, "Slide, slide!" He must make his decision early enough so his players will know how to react.*

Signals

Another important item for the coach is the signal system. Whether the coach gives the signals from a coaching box or from the bench, they must be simple. **Don't worry about the other team stealing your signals.** Worry about your team's ability to handle the system correctly.

The best signals are those given verbally to a youngster before he goes to bat. For example, when the first batter comes up you say "If you get to first, steal second base on the first pitch." Since verbal signals cannot be used all the time, each team must have a signal system. The signal system should have signs that are easy for the youngsters to remember. If the coach is giving signals from the bench he can use the following signs. Steal, touching "steel" poles by the dugout. The bunt signal could be the coach placing his hand on a bat. "Taking" off the cap could mean "take."

If the coach is in the third-base coaching box, he can use simplified signs such as belt for bunt, sock for steal, trousers for take and hat for hit-and-run. Advanced teams usually have a key, a special sign which indicates that further signals will follow. For instance, the hat may mean hit-and-run, but only if the coach is standing in the very front of the coaching box. If touching the hat is the key, and touching the belt means bunt, the bunt signal can only be given after the coach has touched his hat. He may touch his belt all through the game, but it does not count unless he has touched his hat first (Fig. 10-15).

Regardless of the signal system you use, you and your players must follow certain rules to ensure good results. No runner should ever take a signal while standing off a base. Each batter should be out of the batter's box and looking directly at the coach for a signal after each pitch.

The hitters should be taught to wait until you clap your hands before going back into the batter's box. One reason for this is that many youngsters turn away before you can give them the signal. Even more youngsters turn away as soon as you give them the signal. Many youngsters give away the fact that they have received a signal by looking to the next base, grabbing dirt in their hands, or in some cases, looking into the stands for their parents. However, they have gotten the signal. Making them wait until you clap your hands will make them concentrate more. You can, of course, give many fake signals, but nothing too difficult.

Some coaches use an acknowledgment: a signal from the batter, like moving his hand up and down the bat to indicate he received the signal. I believe this is just another signal for the players to remember and is not necessary.

Fig. 10-15. Whatever signal system you decide on, don't worry about the other team stealing the signals. Most teams rarely make the effort to bother with the opposition's signs. Make the signs clear and simple.

A very important signal is the "wipe-off" or "repeat" signal. If a youngster isn't sure of the signal he can rub his hand across his chest, and the coach will repeat the signal, if there was one. If not, the coach rubs his hand across his chest. This indicates that there's nothing on, and if there was, it has now been "wiped off." This communication between players and coaches can cut out all the time-outs used to call boys over and explain about the signal they are not sure of.

General Information

Proper footwear is important for good baserunning. Sporting-goods dealers now have literally dozens of different athletic shoes. Some have metal spikes for baseball, rubber cleats for soccer, and even a special design for traction on boats. Because of the large selection in design and color, most youth-leaguers can obtain the shoes they need without metal spikes and still have the traction they need to play baseball. There is definitely no need to use metal spikes until at least age thirteen. Even at thirteen it is questionable whether the risk of injury is worth the seeming extra traction. Not only can spikes cut another player, but a very common injury occurs when the player gets his own spikes caught in the turf and hurts an ankle or knee. League officials should consider not allowing metal spikes until age fifteen if suitable footwear without metal spikes is available in their area.

Nothing so characterizes youth-league games as the kind of stop-and-go effect where, with the ball in play and the base runners moving, everything stops for a second or two and just as suddenly picks up and continues. The ball seems to follow the lower-division base runner around the diamond, rarely catching up to him.

The aggressive baserunning teams will usually come out on top. Runners taught to seek the extra base and stay alert for the possible overthrow will more often than not find overwhelming success.

XI. Practice Organization and Drills

Practice sessions should be held to improve the players' skills, increase their knowledge of the game, improve their ability to respond to various game situations, and improve player and team morale. Tryout sessions and early-season conditioning are important, but these usually do not take long, and conditioning is later incorporated into the regular-season practice. Too many practice sessions include only batting practice and a round or two of infield and outfield work. Practice sessions are when the coach must teach.

Sound organization demands that a coach decide exactly what he wants to accomplish in each session. He then sets up a schedule of activities and drills. This schedule should be organized so that he may work with individuals or small groups while the remainder of the squad is practicing skills which do not require direct supervision.

Practice sessions have to be arranged so that all the youngsters will have something to do. No one should be standing around. The players should shift from one drill to another. Different drills should be used from time to time to keep up the interest of the boys. As an example, a batter with a poor knowledge of the strike zone could be coupled with a pitcher who is having trouble controlling his pitches. A catcher who needs work on low balls can be coupled with a first baseman who needs work on scooping low throws. A pitcher who needs work on his move to first base can work with baserunners who need work on their leads. Not every player's weakness can be covered, but pointing out individual weaknesses is important. Youngsters are more likely to correct their mistakes and improve on their skills if they really understand which skills they are trying to improve and why.

Repetition is very important. The coach must repeat each point as often as necessary. Boys must practice time and time again, so that during the game they can act intuitively.

While there is no exact practice schedule for all teams to follow, almost every practice session must start by having the boys loosen up. This should be done for about ten minutes. Make sure all the pairs of youngsters throwing to each other are lined up and throwing in the same direction. This is necessary so an overthrow won't hit a teammate. The players should start approximately thirty feet apart and work their way back to sixty feet apart. When they throw, they should pick out a target on their throwing partner and aim for it. This will improve their throwing accuracy.

Batting practice and play situations should be included every day. These drills are so important that they will be explained separately later in this chapter. Batting practice should take about thirty minutes, play situations about twenty minutes. Time should also be set aside for the "skill of the day." Usually twenty minutes is enough. The skill of the day may be sliding one day, the bunting game the next day, and stopping the first-and-third steal another day.

You can't practice a drill once and expect youngsters to learn and remember the skills it emphasizes. You should set up general time limits, but once set up, they should not be too rigid. Don't leave a drill if you feel the players need more work. If time is up, come back to the drill the very next practice, and don't go on to another drill until you feel the youngsters are ready.

After the skill of the day, the coach should divide up the team for team drills. These take about ten minutes. They might include fly balls and ground balls to the outfielders, with special emphasis on balls over their heads. Meanwhile, the infielders can take more ground balls, with special emphasis on slow rollers or on getting the lead runner. The pitchers and any extra players can be used as fungo hitters.

If practice is set up for ten A.M., then it must begin exactly at that time. Don't wait for two or three latecomers. Youngsters with good reasons for coming late or missing practice should not be disciplined. Only when they appear to be taking advantage of the coach and their teammates should they be disciplined. Remember, they're only youngsters; you should not expect them to adhere to rules like older athletes who are on scholarships or getting paid for playing. The punishment must fit the crime. Each youngster is different—you as the coach are the best judge of how to handle each of your players. If you are fair, firm and consistent, you will have no problems.

Youth-league coaches should try to have as many practices as possible in the beginning of the season. After the team is selected and the actual games begin, the number of practice sessions can be cut down.

Never let your players go home without having a short meeting after the practice. Taking about five mienutes, tell them what improvements have been made and which skills need more improvement. Announce the time and date of the next practice. Make sure the boys are seated and quiet before you begin. Be certain they are not facing the sun, or they will not be able to look up at you when you are speaking.

Baseball is one of the most difficult sports to coach. You not only have to teach the specifics of all nine positions, but you have to work offensively as well. You will soon learn that you need help or everyone will be standing around, occasionally chasing a batted ball. Don't be afraid to seek help. If another adult is not available, get help from the team leaders and more experienced boys so your practice sessions will be a positive force in determining the successful outcome of many games.

Batting Practice

Batting practice takes up the majority of practice time. Because the pitchers are wild and the batters are selective, even having only ten players hit takes up more time than the other parts of the practice session. While it is true that all players need more batting practice, they must be encouraged to work on their own.

They don't have to wait until the coach calls practice. In addition to working at home—improving their strength and swinging at imaginary pitches in all parts of the strike zone—upper-division players can get equipment, find a field, and take batting practice on their own.

Batting practice should be well planned to get the most out of the time allowed. Each player must not only know when he bats but how many bunts and swings he is to take. He must also know what to do when he is not hitting. The batting order should be the same for all batting-practice sessions. Once the regular season begins, it is a good idea to use the actual game batting order. The extra players can hit after the first nine players. If the starting players hit in their regular order, they can work on the hit-and-run, squeeze and other offensive plays.

Every batter must use a helmet. Not only is using helmets safer, but the hitters will become accustomed to them and be able to concentrate on hitting. It may be true that batting-practice pitching is softer than game pitching; however, the casualness of batting practice and the inexperience of the pitchers make the helmet a necessity for each batter.

Each batter should go through the correct bunting procedure. He should bunt a man to second base, move him over to third base with another bunt, and bunt a third time for a squeeze play. Check to see that he does not just go through the motions—that he concentrates on laying down three good bunts.

Most high-school or college hitters will take anywhere from ten to thirty swings in batting practice. This is usually done by having each batter hit two or three times per session. Youth-league coaches would be better off not counting the number of swings, but instead allowing each hitter a certain amount of time. Two to four minutes, depending upon whether you as coach feel the hitter has had enough swings and has made enough contact, should be enough time under most circumstances. If only swings are counted, it is possible that many inexperienced hitters will not hit the ball often enough. They may need ten swings to hit it two or three times. It is a better idea to have the hitters take two short rounds of two minutes apiece than one long round of four minutes. If a player only gets one chance at batting practice, he may lose interest while waiting for the rest of the team to hit. Also, though it is not always apparent, hitters often develop tired wrists or shoulders after ten good cuts. Batting practice will not be beneficial if the hitter is not taking a good swing at the ball.

The coach must make sure the hitter recognizes all strikes and swings at them. However, swinging at bad pitches in batting practice can become a bad habit. Have the hitters remain patient. An umpire for batting practice is a good idea, especially if the coach cannot watch each pitch because he is teaching at another part of the field. A reliable player, usually the catcher, can call the pitches. He should try to see that the batter swings at all reasonably good pitches.

Incidentally, don't forget about the young man who catches batting practice. Make sure you change your catcher two or three times. You need not use regular catchers; any confident youngster with reasonable ability can catch batting practice, It is a good idea to let the catchers hit before they catch. This way batting practice will not be held up waiting for a catcher to take off his catching gear in order to bat.

Pitchers should put something on the ball. The pitches will not be the same as in a game, but if the pitcher lobs the ball over, the batter rarely gets anything out of batting practice. The hitter must try to work on all pitches, but in certain drills he should know what pitch is coming. Remember, batting practice is for the hitters; they should gain confidence. If they are unable to hit the ball well, then nothing is accomplished.

The coach should be sure that all the positions in the field are covered. Do not let groups of three or four players get together in the outfield and talk about what show is going to be on "Creature Feature" that night. The coach or some reliable players should fungo balls to the fielders between pitches. The fungo hitter waits until the ball passes the batter; then he hits the ball to one of the fielders.

If all the players are kept moving, batting practice will not drag along. Only the next hitter should be getting his helmet and bat ready; all the others are in their positions on the field, receiving ground balls or fly balls. Players who have just finished hitting should run the bases. They pretend that there is one out and play each batted ball as if they were in an actual game. They can practice all the baserunning situations while their teammates are hitting and fielding.

Batting practice, if conducted properly, can help the youngsters improve not only their hitting but their fielding and baserunning as well. The coach must make every effort to see that batting practice is carried on in such a manner that it will be as valuable as possible for the individual and the team. Organize and plan, supervise and teach; then batting practice will be a positive experience for every team member.

Play Situations

The most important defensive team drill involves play situations. Almost every situation your team's defense will encounter can be covered. The action is fast and very interesting. No players have to wait too long to field, throw or run, as everyone will be involved in the drill. The drill is simple and easy to set up and will be as close to actual game conditions as possible. One reason this drill is so successful is that it is under the direct control of the coach. The entire team is involved; the coach may stop action, correct mistakes and create new situations. The drill should be used in every practice session.

To set up the drill, the coach places a complete fielding team in position; he stands in the batter's box with a fungo bat and a ball. Any extra players line up behind an imaginary line between home plate and the third base dugout. The pitcher delivers a pitch, although he does not throw as hard as in a game. As the ball enters the catcher's mitt, the coach throws his ball up and hits it, just as he would when hitting fungoes. The fielders play the ball as in a regular game. With practice the coach can hit singles, doubles, and fly balls, creating almost any situation he wishes. The first youngster in the running line waits until the coach fungoes the ball and then runs out the ball as he would in an actual game. If a coach has no extra players, he can call out the situation and the number of outs before he fungoes the ball.

Naturally, not every situation can be covered in a single practice session. After some games have been played, the coach will have an idea of which situations need more work. If he feels he is able, he may hit the ball the pitcher throws instead of fungoing the ball he is holding. This limits his ability to hit the ball exactly where he wants it, but it gives the players a more realistic look at the batted ball.

The coach should make sure the players back up every play. There is a place for all nine players to go in every situation. They should also chatter and hustle on every play. After each three outs, clear the bases and start another inning. If no runners are available, call out the situation and the number of outs before each pitch. If you are able to use base runners, make sure they all have helmets. It is not necessary to have the runners slide or dive back to base. Only the execution by the defense is important; whether or not the runner is out is secondary. If possible, someone should coach third base.

Don't let your players handle too many balls. To prevent them from being forced to make too many hard throws for one day, substitute liberally, playing some youngsters at more than one position. While this drill is primarily designed to help each youngster at his specific position, the entire team will gain confidence. The base runners can also be corrected if they do something wrong. You may also want them to get intentionally picked off or miss a base to see if the defense is alert.

It is the coach's job to prepare every player at each position for any situation that may come up in a game. If the youngster has not practiced a situation, he cannot be expected to handle it correctly in a game. Outfield throws to the cutoff men, rundowns, getting the lead runner and thinking ahead are all parts of this drill. If this drill is used properly, as often as possible, and with the necessary changes in personnel, your team will be prepared for its opponents in the easiest and best possible way.

Other Drills and Suggestions

Pepper is one of the oldest drills in the game, and it is still beneficial to fielders and batters. The drill usually uses one batter and no more than three fielders. The batter attempts to hit each fielder a ground ball from about twenty feet away. After fifteen balls have been hit, the players rotate. This is a good drill, but there is an even better method of playing pepper. I call it "elongated pepper." It uses a batter, a pitcher about twenty feet away, a catcher about fifteen feet behind the batter and an outfielder (Fig. 11-1). The idea is for the batter to hit every ball back to the pitcher. However, many times the pitch is too hard to reach or the batter mistakenly hits it past the pitcher. The catcher and fielder return the ball quickly to the pitcher so that the drill can continue. Let each batter hit for two minutes, then rotate until all the players have batted and played the other three positions.

Another drill, called "pick-ups," is a great conditioner. The players pair off. One member of each pair rolls the ball to the other, who fields and returns it. The first roll is about ten feet to the fielder's left, the second about ten feet to his right (Fig. 11-2). This is repeated about twenty-five times. The players then switch positions.

A great fielding drill is the backboard drill. The player simply throws a "rag" ball or rubber ball against a wall and fields it.

An excellent team batting drill is "shadow swings." The coach should line up his entire team in three lines, leaving enough room for

Fig. 11-1. *"Elongated pepper" is a great early season drill. It provides practice for the batter in keeping his eye on the ball and gives each fielder practice as well. This method of pepper keeps the game moving quickly, as every ball is played by someone.*

Fig. 11-2. *"Pick-ups" is an excellent conditioner. Each player does up to twenty-five, then switches with a teammate.*

them to swing their bats. They take their normal batting stances and the coach calls out a pitch: "Outside corner, knee high, ready, swing." All the players take a game-type swing at that pitch. The coach calls out other pitches and the players practice their swings. The coach can also work on other actions, like getting out of the way of a pitch or taking a pitch. This drill also provides an excellent opportunity for the coach to go over the signals and make sure every player on his team knows exactly what to do when he is up at bat (Fig. 11-3).

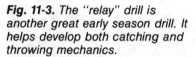

Fig. 11-3. *The "relay" drill is another great early season drill. It helps develop both catching and throwing mechanics.*

If things get dull at practice, there are many ways for a coach to liven up the practice session. He might try a baseball track meet. Lower-division players really love relay races and races around the bases. If a stop watch is not available, have two players start at home plate, one facing third and the other facing first. They both break on your starting signal, and the winner is the boy who gets back to home plate first. To avoid a collision at second, the runner going by way of third touches the inside portion of the base and the runner going via first touches the outside portion.

Baseball golf is a lot of fun. Using a bat and ball, have the players see how many strokes are necessary to putt the baseball from home plate until the ball touches first base. Have them continue to second and third, counting the total number of strokes.

If you have a movie or video camera, record the boys at practice and point out their mistakes at a meeting. The meeting can be at night at someone's home where refreshments can be served. This serves not only as a classroom session of instruction but a social event as well. You can also use still photographs. While they are not always as good as moving pictures for helping locate coaching points, they can be a valuable teaching tool, and the youngsters and parents will like to have them as souvenirs.

A laboratory approach to watching a baseball game is another way of teaching youngsters and having a fine social event as well. Take your team to a local college or professional ball game and critically watch it, pointing out all the mistakes and good plays. Tell the boys this is a learning experience as well as entertainment. Move around from player to player and make sure each one is watching his position in the field.

Capitalizing on mistakes and exceptional plays made by opponents is a great teaching tool. Have your boys take notes during each ball game. One player can be charting pitchers and hitters while another watches the moves of as many opposing players as possible. When the game is over, the coach collects the notes to be used at a team meeting the next practice session. Players will quickly find that watching other players can be an excellent learning experience. They may find that the best hitter on the other team usually hits the first pitch or rarely swings at bad pitches. They may find that the poor fielders are not staying down on ground balls or are not trying to get the best hop. A player who is not in the game at the time can be kept busy and contribute to the team even without getting a hit that day. He may be the one who notices something during the game that can help a teammate improve his skill in some phase of the game.

A coach should always use a mental-error book. He should write down every mental mistake that happens in a game. (Physical mistakes need not be listed.) These include not calling for a pop fly, not backing up a base, making an unnecessary throw, missing a signal, etc., etc. The mental-error book should also include all the good points of the game. A coach can have his manager or one of the boys not playing help him keep the mental-error book. If the team wins, it is a good idea to go into the outfield, sit down, and discuss all the items in the mental-error book. If the team loses, wait until the next practice session or before the next game to go over the book. You will soon find players volunteering information for the book. You and your players can include plays by the other team as good and bad examples. You may think you can remember all the items in the game, but writing them down as they happen is the only sure way (Fig. 11-4).

Fig. 11-4. The coach should write down all the mistakes made during the game. He should go over them right after the game if his team wins. If they lose he should wait until the next practice session.

Whenever I think of practice and drills I think of the following poem, reprinted with the permission of Danny Litwhiler, baseball coach at Michigan State University and author of the book, *Baseball Coach's Guide to Drills and Skills.* Enjoy the poem, enjoy practice and the games. But most of all, win or lose, enjoy the youngsters, for they are what coaching is all about.

Drills, Drills, Drills!

The baseball coach was mighty tough,
He never seemed to get enough
Of drill, and drill, and drill and drill,
Until it seemed he wished to kill.
The players made a lot of fuss,
And said, "He's making fools of us.
Now what's the use of all that stuff?
We know those plays all well enough.
If he would let us play a game,
We'd use those plays just the same."
At last there came the longed-for day
When they had THE big game to play.
And then those weeks of constant drill
Began to show in baseball skill.
The team would make their double plays
And shine in lots of other ways.
They'd catch a runner off at first
The way they often had rehearsed.
And if one tried a hit to stretch
They always got the sorry wretch.
And when they came to bat themselves,
They acted like some sprightly elves.
They made their double steals with ease,
And did about just as they'd please.
They bunted in a man from third,
And made the pitcher look absurd.
And when the game was played and won,
They said, "Oh boy, but that was fun.
Hey, Coach, we want to drill some more,
And next time make a bigger score."

By RAYMOND F. BELLAMY

Each coach must sincerely love the game. Encourage your boys to play baseball as long as they can. Make them work hard but have fun too. They probably won't be among the chosen few who make the major leagues, but years later when they are seated behind desks, working in stores or doing whatever their professions might require, they will remember timely base hits, happy victories and, yes, heartbreaking defeats. They will remember their teammates, and, most of all, they'll remember **the coach.**

SPORTS PUBLISHER

MASTERS PRESS

A Division of Howard W. Sams & Co.

Spalding Youth League Series:

Youth, Sports & Self Esteem
Darrell J. Burnett, Ph. D.

Dr. Burnett, a clinical child psychologist, offers parents 12 specific guidelines for promoting their kids' self esteem through youth sports. A skills section teaches basic skills for basketball, football, soccer, and baseball/softball.

> 160 pages ■ 5 1/4 X 8 1/4
> 0-940279-80-0 ■ $12.95
> b/w photos
> paper

Youth League Basketball
Joe Williams & Stan Wilson

Demonstrates effective ways to teach the fundamental skills and strategies that players of all ages must master to excel in basketball. Emphasizes teamwork and unselfish play.

> 128 pages ■ 5 1/4 X 8 1/4
> 0-940279-70-3 ■ $9.95
> b/w photos
> paper

Youth League Football
Tom Flores & Bob O'Connor

Drills and coaching suggestions for all positions on the field, along with equipment information and hints for keeping the emphasis on "play" rather than "work".

> 192 pages ■ 5 1/4 X 8 1/4
> 0-940279-69-X ■ $12.95
> b/w photos
> paper

Youth League Soccer

A complete handbook for coaches that focuses on such important issues as conducting practice, inspiring young players, first-aid, and coaching during a game.

> 192 pages ■ 5 1/4 X 8 1/4
> 0-940279-47-9 ■ $9.95
> b/w photos
> paper

All Masters Press titles, including those in the Youth League Series, are available in bookstores or by calling (800) 722-2677.

Fault-Correction Index

CATCHING

Breaks the webbing of his mitt frequently, 11
Catches the ball with one hand, 17
Catches too far from the hitter, 16
Doesn't back up bases, 31
Drops too many foul-tips, 17
Drops too many pitches, 17
Fields bunts poorly, 31
Gives signs improperly, 14
Grips the ball improperly, 22
Hand frequently bruised, 12
Hit with foul-tip on the meat hand frequently, 16
Improper footwork when throwing to the bases, 26
Improper mitt, 11
Improper player selection, 11, 33
Improper protective equipment, 13
Lack of communication using pick-off plays, 14
Misses too many low balls, 17, 20
Misses too many pop flies, 30
Opposition stealing signals, 14
Poor crouch position, 15
Poor relationship with umpires, 32
Scarcity of catchers, 11
Shuts his eyes when the ball is hit, 13
Stopping the first and third steal, 27
Takes too long to throw, 23, 26
Throwing, 22
Throwing arm is physically weak, 23
Throwing sidearm, 23
Too many collisions at home plate, 28

FIRST BASE

Backs up bases poorly, 67
Commits himself too soon on pop flies, 65

Commits himself too soon on throws to first base, 58
Commits himself too soon on balls hit to his right, 62
Fields bunts poorly, 63
Fields ground balls poorly, 62
Holds runners on poorly, 64
Improper glove, 57
Improper player selection, 57
Misses throws from the catcher, 61
Misses too many low throws, 59
Not watching to see if the runner touches first base, 69
Poor positioning, 58
Poor positioning of anticipation, 58
Tags runner improperly, 59, 64
Tags the base improperly, gets stepped on often, 58, 59
Throws are inaccurate, 68
Throwing arm is physically weak, 23, 47

PITCHING

Arm injured, 47
Bends over too much when taking signs, 37
Can't see signals, 14
Change-up is poor, 51
Control is poor, 39, 40, 41, 46
Curve ball is thrown improperly, 49
Fastball is too straight, doesn't rotate properly, 41
Has trouble holding runners on, 42, 43
Improper fielding, 45
    backing up bases, 46
    bunts, 45
    covering first, 45
    covering home, 46
Inconsistent point to release, 40
Loses his rhythm, 41
Not warming up enough, does poorly in the first inning, 52
Opens up his hip too much, 39
Opposition reads his pitches, 38
Pitches on top of the rubber, 37
    can't push off the rubber,
Pitchout is poor, 52
Poor physical condition, 53
Rushes his delivery, 39, 47
Stopping the first and third steal, 27
Squeeze play defense is poor, 44

Takes his eyes off the target, 38
Throws across his body, 39
Throwing arm is physically weak, 47
Throws sidearm, 40

THIRD BASE

Bunt defense is poor, 76, 77
Catches with one hand, 83
Doesn't know his pick-off plays, 79, 80
Doesn't know when to back up, 78, 79
Doesn't know which pop flies he should take, 79
Improper glove, 72
Improper positioning, 72, 73
Lets the ball play him, 80
    doesn't get the good hop,
Picks up the slow roller improperly, 80
Tags the runner too high, 77, 78
Takes too many steps when throwing to a base, 79, 80
Throws from first base to the pitcher get by, 79, 80
Throwing inaccurately, 23, 83
Throwing arm is physically weak, 23, 47
Trouble with the first and third steal, 27

SECOND BASE

Catches with one hand, 83
Doesn't back up pitcher, 91
Doesn't know which pop flies are his, 113
Doesn';t use the double cutoff, 89
Double play, 88
    pivots too much, 88
    throws too hard to the shortstop, 88
Fields ground balls poorly, 85, 86
Fields the slow roller poorly, 85, 86
Holds the ball too long in a run-down, 90, 91
Improper positioning, 85, 86
Improper position of anticipation, 85, 86
Improper run-down procedure, 90, 91
Leaves his position too soon to cover the base on a steal, 88
Not covering first base on a bunt attempt, 92
Stopping the double steal, 27
Tags runners too high, 88

Throws are inaccurate, 22, 46
Throwing arm is physically weak, 23, 47

OUTFIELD

Back pedals after the ball, 110
Catchable balls drop between fielders, 112
Catchers the ball below eye level, 110
Doesn't play the wind, 110
Drifts after the ball, 110
Fly balls appear to be moving up and down while
    chasing after them, 110
Ground balls get by fielders, 114
Improper player selection, 107, 116
Loses ball in the sun, 115, 116
Plays too deep, 109
Poor footwork in taking off after a fly ball, 115, 116
Poor positioning, 108, 109
Throws to the infield are usually too high, 78, 115, 116
Throws to the infield usually tail off, 114
Trouble playing a fence or a wall, 115

HITTING

Afraid of the ball, 126
Arms too far away from body, 123
Arms too rigid, 123
Batting practice takes too long, 169, 170
Can't get out of the way of a pitch, 126
Cradles the bat, 122
Doesn't watch the ball hit the bat, 128
Guess-hits, 134, 135
Hips are locked in, 132, 133
Improper bat, 120
Improper grip, 120
Improper stance, 120
Lunges at the ball, 124
On deck hitter not prepared, 136
Physically weak batter, 135, 136
Pulls his head out too soon, 128
Rarely hits the ball to the opposite field, 132
Steps in the bucket, 128
Strides too far, 126

Sweeps at the ball, 132
Swings at bad pitches, 134
Swings from the end of the bat, 123
Swings too hard, 123
Uppercuts at the pitch, 125
Weight too far back on the heels, 128

SHORTSTOP

Catches the ball with one hand, 83
Can't reach balls hit to either side, 97, 99
Doesn't know what to do when a runner misses a base, 102
Errors a ball and gets frustrated, 103
Fields ground balls poorly,
 fielded too far beneath him, 97
 slow roller, 85, 86
Improper positioning, 95, 96
Improper position of anticipation, 95, 96
Improper run-down procedure, 90, 91
Lets ball play him, 104, 105
Misplays pop flies, 103, 113
Poor communication, 101, 102
Poor position as cutoff man, 103
Stopping the first and third steal, 27, 104
Tags runners too high, 88
Takes too many steps before he releases the ball, 79, 80
Throws are inaccurate, 22, 46
Throwing arm is physically weak, 23, 47
Trouble with the double play, 100
 doesn't touch the base, 101
 not in position for the throw, 100

BASE RUNNING

Can't get a jump on the pitcher, 153
Caught by hidden ball trick, 149
Caught by left-handed pitcher at first, 150
Coach and base runners have trouble communicating, 160, 161
Crosses his legs while leading off first base, 148
Doesn't turn at first base well when going for extra bases, 151
Doesn't shiffle off base after each pitch, 150
Jumps at first base on close plays, 147
Places hands on knees while leading off base, 149

Poor start from home plate, 146
Running form is poor, 146
Runs too far down the line while leading off thrid base, 154
Slides poorly, 154
      too close to the base, 155
Trouble with shoes, 164
Trouble with signals, 162, 163
Trouble tagging up, 152, 153

BUNTING

Ball is hit too hard, 139
Poor grip, 138
Pops up most attempts, 140
Squares around too far back in the batter's box, 140
Youngsters don't like to bunt, 142